CERTIFICATION AND SECURITY IN INTER-ORGANIZATIONAL E-SERVICES

IFIP – The International Federation for Information Processing

IFIP was founded in 1960 under the auspices of UNESCO, following the First World Computer Congress held in Paris the previous year. An umbrella organization for societies working in information processing, IFIP's aim is two-fold: to support information processing within its member countries and to encourage technology transfer to developing nations. As its mission statement clearly states,

> *IFIP's mission is to be the leading, truly international, apolitical organization which encourages and assists in the development, exploitation and application of information technology for the benefit of all people.*

IFIP is a non-profitmaking organization, run almost solely by 2500 volunteers. It operates through a number of technical committees, which organize events and publications. IFIP's events range from an international congress to local seminars, but the most important are:

• The IFIP World Computer Congress, held every second year;
• Open conferences;
• Working conferences.

The flagship event is the IFIP World Computer Congress, at which both invited and contributed papers are presented. Contributed papers are rigorously refereed and the rejection rate is high.

As with the Congress, participation in the open conferences is open to all and papers may be invited or submitted. Again, submitted papers are stringently refereed.

The working conferences are structured differently. They are usually run by a working group and attendance is small and by invitation only. Their purpose is to create an atmosphere conducive to innovation and development. Refereeing is less rigorous and papers are subjected to extensive group discussion.

Publications arising from IFIP events vary. The papers presented at the IFIP World Computer Congress and at open conferences are published as conference proceedings, while the results of the working conferences are often published as collections of selected and edited papers.

Any national society whose primary activity is in information may apply to become a full member of IFIP, although full membership is restricted to one society per country. Full members are entitled to vote at the annual General Assembly, National societies preferring a less committed involvement may apply for associate or corresponding membership. Associate members enjoy the same benefits as full members, but without voting rights. Corresponding members are not represented in IFIP bodies. Affiliated membership is open to non-national societies, and individual and honorary membership schemes are also offered.

CERTIFICATION AND SECURITY IN INTER-ORGANIZATIONAL E-SERVICES

IFIP TC-11 Second International Workshop on Certification and Security in Inter-Organizational E-Services (CSES), World Computer Congress, Aug. 22-27, 2004, Toulouse, France

Edited by

Enrico Nardelli
NESTOR – Laboratorio Sperimental per la Sicurezza e la Certificazione of Servizi Telematici Multimediali, University of Rome "Tor Vergata"
Italy

Maurizio Talamo
NESTOR – Laboratorio Sperimental per la Sicurezza e la Certificazione of Servizi Telematici Multimediali, University of Rome "Tor Vergata"
Italy

 Springer

Library of Congress Cataloging-in-Publication Data

A C.I.P. Catalogue record for this book is available from the Library of Congress.

Certification and Security in Inter-Organizational E-Services Edited by Enrico Nardelli and Maurizio Talamo

 p.cm. (The International Federation for Information Processing)

 ISBN: 1-4614-9809-0 / (eBOOK) 0-387-25088-3 Printed on acid-free paper.

9 8 7 6 5 4 3 2 1   SPIN 11397427 (HC) / 11397458 (eBook)
springeronline.com

Contents

Preface

This volume contains the final proceedings of CSES-04, the 2nd International Workshop on Certification and Security in Inter-Organizational E-Services, held on 26-27 August 2004 in Toulouse (France) within the IFIP World Computer Congress 2004.

The objective of the workshop was to discuss technical and organizational aspects regarding the areas of certification and of security in network services and their interrelations, presenting both real-life application experiences and methodological proposals, from participants belonging to the governmental, industrial and academic communities.

The program of the workshop featured four sessions with contributed papers, selected by the international program committee on the basis of their scientific quality and relevance for the workshop topics. On the basis of the committee evaluation of papers, 12 submissions have been selected for presentation at CSES-04 workshop, 9 as full papers (30 minutes for presentation) and 3 as short papers (15 minutes for presentation and limited to 6 pages in the proceedings). There were an overall 20 submissions, a larger than 1/3 increase from the 14 submissions of the first edition of CSES, in 2002 in Montreal. A very good result, with such a large number of competing events in this area. 8 submissions failed to qualify as of some interest (in scope and/or in quality) for the workshop and were rejected. 2 of the accepted papers were not presented at the workshop, hence they have not been included in this volume of proceedings. These proceedings also feature an up-to-date account of the current state of deployoment of the Italian Electronic Identity Card, one of the most advanced national efforts in the area of electronic authentication of citizens.

The CSES-04 program also featured two panels, a first one examining trust management models from different perspectives (information security, agent systems, . . .), and a second one discussing from an industrial viewpoint major trust and security challenges for business centric Virtual Organizations. Panels were organized jointly with the co-located FAST (Formal Aspect in Security and Trust) workshop.

ENRICO NARDELLI AND MAURIZIO TALAMO

WORKSHOP ORGANIZATION

Program Committee Chairs

Enrico Nardelli (NESTOR - Univ. of Rome "Tor Vergata", Italy) Co-Chair
Maurizio Talamo (NESTOR - Univ. of Rome "Tor Vergata", Italy) Co-Chair

Sponsoring Institution

IFIP TC 11

Program Committee

Franco Arcieri (NESTOR - Univ. of Rome "Tor Vergata", Italy)
Boualem Benatallah (Univ. of New South Wales, Australia)
Elisa Bertino (Univ. of Milano, Italy)
Athman Bouguettaya (Virginia Tech, USA)
Fabio Casati (HP Labs, USA)
Anindya Datta (Chutney Technologies and Georgia Tech, USA)
Umesh Dayal (HP Labs, USA)
Fabio Fioravanti (Univ. of L'Aquila, Italy)
Giorgio Gambosi (Univ. of Rome "Tor Vergata", Italy)
Bezalel Gavish (Southern Methodist Univ. of, Australia)
Roberto Gorrieri (Univ. of Bologna, Italy)
Paul Grefen (Eindhoven Univ. of Technology, The Netherlands)
Alfons Kemper (Univ. of Passau, Germany)
Norihisa Komoda (Univ. of Osaka, Japan)
Domenico Laforenza (ISTI-CNR, Italia)
Guido Marinelli (NESTOR - Univ. of Rome "Tor Vergata", Italy)
Mike Papazoglou (Univ. of Tilburg, The Netherlands)
Pierangela Samarati (Univ. of Milano, Italy)
Leon Strous (De Nederlandsche Bank, The Netherlands)
Roland Traunmuller (Univ. of Linz, Austria)
Ugo Vaccaro (Univ. of Salerno, Italy)
Marco Vanneschi (Univ. of Pisa, Italy)

Anthony Watson (Edith Watson Univ., Australia)
Gerhard Weikum (Univ. of Saarland, Germany)
Yanchun Zhang (Victoria Univ., Australia)
Yuliang Zheng (Univ. of North Carolina at Charlotte, USA)

Organizing Committee

Andrea Dimitri (NESTOR - Univ. of Rome "Tor Vergata", Italy)
Angelica Fruguglietti (NESTOR - Univ. of Rome "Tor Vergata", Italy)
Daniela Merella (NESTOR - Univ. of Rome "Tor Vergata", Italy)

Acknowledgements

We thank the organizing committee of the IFIP World Computer Congress for their support and especially for the local arrangements in Toulouse. We also thank the organizing committee of CSES 2004 Workshop for their contribution.

This work has been partially supported by the Grant MIUR L.449/97, CNR Project "P1 - INTERNET networks: efficiency, integration and security", Research Action "Security Services" and by the Grant MIUR PNR 2001-2003, FIRB Project RBNE01KNFP "GRID.IT: Enabling Platforms for High-Performance Computational Grids Oriented to Scalable Virtual Organizations".

Special thanks to NESTOR, the "Laboratorio Sperimentale per la Sicurezza e la Certificazione di Servizi Telematici Multimediali" of the University of Rome "Tor Vergata" for its financial support in the preparation and organization of the workshop.

Finally, many thanks to Fabio Fioravanti for his invaluable help in the preparation of this volume.

Introduction

The objective of the 2nd International Workshop on Certification and Security in Inter-Organizational E-Services (CSES-04) was to discuss technical and organizational aspects regarding the two interrelated areas of certification and security of e-services, presenting both real-life application experiences and methodological proposals, from participants belonging to the governmental, industrial and academic communities.

The field of services managed and accessed through communication networks is, in fact, growing in magnitude throughout society. A crucial aspect of this process is the capability of certifying what has occurred in the interaction over the networks, and ensuring that the integrity of the involved computer-based systems was maintained. This is even more important given the uptake of distributed computational infrastructure oriented to service provision, like Web-Services and Grid.

Certifying the execution of an e-service provided on the network as the result of the interaction among independent organizations is a critical area for the underlying IT-infrastructure. In fact, given the legal value that is often attached to data managed and exchanged during the execution of such an inter-organizational e-service, being able to document what was actually carried out is of the utmost importance. This is made more complex in cases where e- services are based on legacy systems managed by autonomous and independent organizations, as often happens in the public administration sector.

Additionally, the whole area of security issues, from the basic (availability, authentication, integrity, confidentiality) to the more complex (e.g., authorization, non-repudiation) involves the equally critical ability to track down responsibilities ("who did what"). This capability is mandatory to increase the presence and use of e-service IT-infrastructures.

The two areas of certification and security have therefore a common technological intersection, since both are based on the reliable and efficient monitoring of executed and running processes. Monitoring requires the capability of tracing and analyzing what is going on in the distributed system and in the underlying IT-infrastructure. Monitoring is also important for contractual and quality reasons, i.e. to serve as a basis for checking the respect of obligation and duties and the value of performance levels.

Certification and security are as well fundamental processes in organizational and economic terms. Organizationally, they support an easier cooperation between autonomous and independent organizations in the building of a new complex service to be made available in the electronic marketplace. In fact, they allow to build this new cooperative service without having each involved organization fear to lose their control and their influence on its core business and on application fields it knows better. Moreover, by allowing to clearly pinpoint responsibilities in the cooperation they enable a more efficient management of organizational interactions. Economically, they make it possible, for example, to provide and effectively manage value-added services with many different "options", supplying different service levels with different fees. Additionally, they support the substitutions of providers of basic services, thus fostering economic competition and quality level improvements.

Certification and security are also two foundation stones on which to base the realization of more advanced e-services obtained by composition of more elementary ones. In fact, operating at the immaterial level of electronic technologies is easier to combine and integrate existing services to provide new and better ones. But, since systems providing advanced e-services are based on a complex interaction among many large IT systems higher risks of failure are possible due to the lower degree of system reliability that newest information and telecommunication technologies have.

THE ITALIAN ELECTRONIC IDENTITY CARD: OVERALL ARCHITECTURE AND IT INFRASTRUCTURE

Franco Arcieri[1], Mario Ciclosi[2], Andrea Dimitri[1], Fabio Fioravanti[1,3], Enrico Nardelli[1] and Maurizio Talamo[1]

[1]*NESTOR - Laboratorio Sperimentale per la Sicurezza e la Certificazione di Servizi Telematici Multimediali - Univ. of Roma "Tor Vergata", Roma, Italia.*

[2]*Direzione Centrale per i Servizi Demografici - Ministero dell'Interno, Roma, Italia.*

[3]*Dipartimento di Informatica, Univ. of L'Aquila, L'Aquila, Italia.*

Abstract

In this paper we describe the overall process of deployment of the Italian Electronic Identity Card: the way it is issued, services it is used for, organizations involved in the process, and the Information Technology (IT) infrastructure enabling the effective management of the whole process while ensuring the mandatory security functions. Organizational complexity lies in the distribution of responsibilities for the management of Personal Data Registries (on which identity of people is based) which is an institutional duty of the more than 8000 Italian municipalities, and the need of keeping a centralized control on all processes dealing with identity of people as prescribed by laws and for national security and police purposes. Technical complexity stems from the need of efficiently supporting this distribution of responsibilities while ensuring, at the same time, interoperability of IT-based systems independent of technical choices of the organizations involved, and fulfilment of privacy constraints. The IT architecture defined for this purpose features a clear separation between security services, provided at an infrastructure level, and application services, exposed on the Internet as Web Services. This approach has allowed to easily design and implement secure interoperability, since - notwithstanding the huge variety of IT solutions deployed all over the Italian Municipalities to manage Personal Data Registries - existing application services have not required major changes to be able to interoperate.

Keywords: IT-Enabled Government Operations

1. Introduction

One of the greatest challenges of digital government research, consists in allowing citizens to access digital government services, while ensuring the best possible security levels both to service providers and to citizens. Guaranteeing security during provision of digital government services is of the outmost importance [ElMI01, JGA+01] as it deals with people identity and rights, and is essential for maintaining collective security.

The success of all digital government services strongly depends on how citizens' identification is performed. Indeed, in case of failure of the mechanisms used for identification of citizens, not only it may become impossible to provide a given service, but there could be a leak of highly sensitive identity data, thus making it easier to steal someone else's identity. This crime, known as identity theft, is becoming more and more common on the network.

The solution which is being followed in Italy for identifying citizens accessing digital government services is based on the Electronic Identity Card.

The Electronic Identity Card (EIC, for short) is a polycarbonate smart card equipped with a microchip (supporting cryptographic functions), and a laser band (featuring an embedded hologram). It contains personal (e.g. name, surname, date of birth,...) and biometric data (photo and fingerprint) of a citizen.

The EIC can serve two different purposes: (i) it can be used as a replacement of the paper based ID-card, and (ii) can be used as an authentication credential, allowing access to network enabled government services. For example, citizens could use their EIC for accessing a municipality's web site allowing them the following operations: generation of self-certified documents, online tax payment, access to administrative databases, online applications and many other. Any public administration or agency which wants to give access to online services to citizens using the EIC, must register at the Ministry of the Interior. In this way, it is possible to guard citizens' rights as well as those of the service provider, as needed in a digital government system.

In this paper we describe the architectural solution we have identified and adopted in Italy to manage the process by which Electronic Identity Cards are issued to citizens. Many organizations are involved in this project: the Italian Ministry of Interior has the ownership and management of the overall project, University of Rome "Tor Vergata" is the technical coordinator of the project, the Italian mint, Istituto Poligrafico e Zecca dello Stato (IPZS), manufactures and initializes EICs, the Central Directorate for Demographic Services of the Ministry of Interior (CNSD) is responsible for validating personal data to be written on EICs, and the security system of the EICs architecture, Sistema di Sicurezza della CIE (SSCE), generates keys used for activating EICs and is responsible for guaranteeing security during the formation of data and issue of EICs.

The problem of guaranteeing security in complex services, gets harder when independent agencies play different roles in service provision, as it happens with EIC. In these cases, the responsibility for correctness of service provision is distributed among all organization involved in the process. At the same time, it extremely important to be able to identify culprits of failure in service provision, as often there is a legal and economic value associated to a service. As already pointed out, in the EIC specific case, any information leak can compromise individual as well as collective security.

Any technical solution which is to be used for ensuring secure interoperability among systems from independent organizations, should feature low invasiveness with respect to locally deployed technological solutions and organizational policies.

The paper is structured as follows. In Section 2, we present the reference scenario and requirements for issuing Electronic Identity Cards in Italy. Then, in Section 3, we discuss the adopted solution from an organizational viewpoint. Next, in Section 4 we describe the deployment of the architecture for the Italian Electronic Identity Card, and in Section 5 we describe our approach to security services provision.

2.   Management of Personal Data in Italy

In Italy, municipalities are responsible for maintaining an archive of personal data of people having established residence within the Municipality's territory (APR = Anagrafe della Popolazione Residente) and an archive of former resident people having now established residence outside Italy (AIRE = Anagrafe degli Italiani Residenti all'Estero).

A person is inserted into a Municipality's APR when is born or establishes the residence in its territory. A person is deleted from a Municipality's APR when dies or establishes the residence outside its territory: in the case the residence is established outside Italy, a record is inserted into Municipality's AIRE.

The Ministry of Interior has the overall responsibility for the correct maintenance of Personal Data Registries (APR and AIRE) in all Italian Municipalities. In order to understand the dimensions of the problem, it is important to note the variety in size and complexity of these archives, since about 6000 of the 8192 Italian Municipalities have less then 5000 citizens, but 8 of the 20 Region chief towns have more than one million inhabitants.

In many administrative processes regarding citizens managed by a Public Administration (PA) there is the need, for the organization managing the process, to obtain a certified declaration relative to citizen's personal data. Clearly, for facts regarding birth place and date, residence and civil state, this is responsibility of the Municipality where a person has established the residence.

Moreover, databases containing people's personal data are subject to a severe privacy legislation, forbidding to any public or private organization to set-up and maintain - even temporarily - databases storing personal facts about people unless this is done to discharge a precise obligation settled by law. Also, any maintenance and processing operation on databases storing people's personal data has to be traced both in terms of the operating machine executing it and of the user controlling it.

Hence any approach based on establishing and using a central repository for people's personal data was unlawful - notwithstanding its technical feasibility, and any approach based on changing current legislation to centralize responsibility was bound to failure, given the understandable desire of various organizations to keep their autonomy and their responsibilities.

In moving from a paper-based ID card to an electronic one it was therefore required to define IT-based mechanisms ensuring to the highest degree all IT security functions (confidentiality, integrity, source and destination authentication, authorization, non-repudiation) in the interaction between Municipalities and the Ministry of Interior, and supporting the auditing of interactions. These IT-based mechanisms have to enable the distribution of updates to people's personal data between Municipalities and other PAs, and to ensure certainty of the source authority for exchanged data and security of communication.

Required security functions are the standard basic ones:

- confidentiality: none on the network beyond the communicating parties has to receive data they have exchanged;

- integrity: the destination has to receive exactly the data the source intended to send it;

- source authentication: the destination has to be sure that who is sending the data is the intended source;

- destination authentication: the source has to be sure that who is receiving the data is the intended destination;

- users and machines at the sites of both the communicating parties have to have the prescribed authorization;

- all exchanges of relevant data have to be traced for documentation and certification purposes, to be able to identify, in case of any failure, who was able to properly discharge his/her obligations.

Note that a critical point regarding the above functions is that there is the need of clearly distinguishing data relevant for security functions from data needed for a correct execution of the administrative processes. Too often, in fact, applications dealing with office procedures have to improperly manage also some of the security functions (e.g., authentication and authorization): the result is a bad mix-up between data serving different purposes, making maintenance of these applications more complex and exposing them to higher risks of introducing security flaws.

Any technical solution, moreover, had to be implementable even by small Municipalities without disrupting their work organization and their IT systems and strategies. Indeed, the real obstacle for the true uptake of whichever IT solution one could devise is not the financial cost, but is the organizational impact both in the short term and in the long run.

3.   INA and CNSD

Our approach has been conceptually based on an architectural solution, the so-called Access Keys Warehouse [ACM+01, ACN+99b, ACN+02, AMN+01] (AKW, for short) which was devised while working on similar issues in the context of the interaction of PAs. The AKW approach allows to define and implement IT systems able to keep aligned data referring to the same reality of interest but stored and managed in different and independent PAs, without violating their organizational and technical autonomy [ACN+99a, ACN+01a, ACN+01b, ACN+01c].

Hence, for this case dealing with people's personal data, the organizational component of our solution defined a single access index to the Municipality responsible for one's personal data (INA = Indice Nazionale delle Anagrafi). This index, whose institution was established by a supplement [Law26] to the ordinary law regulating the Personal Data Registries kept in Municipalities [Law1228], provides - for a given person - the reference to the Municipality responsible for his/her personal data. Uniqueness of reference to a person is ensured by using fiscal code as INA's access key.

Therefore, INA is not a central database of the Italian population but simply a provider of the reference to the place where information about a specific person can be found and a means of ensuring overall coherence of the distributed system.

All Municipalities are obliged to communicate to INA any change of established residence for any person in its own territory, and INA keeps under control the overall coherence of Personal Data Registries by rising exceptions whenever an incoherence is detected.

All PAs needing to know or to validate personal data about a given person can first access INA to know which is the responsible Municipality and then obtain directly by such a Municipality required data. In such a way an organization can keep its internal databases up-to-date with respect to changes happening in the real-life without violation to the privacy legislation.

Clearly, since INA is the "leverage point" for the coherence maintenance of the overall distributed system, it is then absolutely necessary to guarantee accuracy of its stored data. Therefore, before the insertion in INA of any piece of information about a person by a Municipality, all elementary components of personal data about such a person have to be verified.

This is easy for what regards the personal data components (e.g., name, birthdate, . . .), since this is competence of the Municipality itself, but for the fiscal code component, this requires an interaction with the Ministry of Finance to verify the current value of fiscal code stored in a Municipality's database and eventually obtain the correct one.

This "data cleaning" activity of information contained in a Municipality's database is a very critical step, like it often happens when operating a recon-ciliation on data coming from different sources [TCDE00]. In our case, the about 10-20% of data referring to the same subject in the reality of interest but differently recorded in different organizations, have been cleaned by means of direct human checking, executed by Municipalities. Since our system is based on the AKW approach [ACM$^+$01, ACN$^+$99b, ACN$^+$02, AMN$^+$01], there is the guarantee that in the future data elements will keep their alignment, hence this is a one-time cost.

Organizational competence for management of INA and of its services towards Municipalities and PAs was given to the National Center for Demographic Ser-vices (CNSD = Centro Nazionale Servizi Demografici) a newly established or-ganizational unit of the Ministry of Interior [MD02]. CNSD is responsible for both the IT infrastructure supporting access to and management of INA and its services and for the end-user support in the utilization of its services. CNSD is also responsible for the management of telematics infrastructure ensuring secure and certified access to its services to all organizations. Technical so-lutions able to implement efficient and effective IT systems to support CNSD activities were devised and tuned by NESTOR Laboratory.

The presence of CNSD means that the logical topology of communication is star-shaped, in the sense that there is not a physical exchange of messages directly between two Municipalities (e.g. when a person moves her estab-lished residence from a Municipality to a different one), or between a PA and a Municipality (e.g. when the Ministry of Health wishes to check a person's es-tablished residence), but CNSD is the control center ensuring official character to these requests.

4.   The Architecture for the Italian Electronic Identity Card

In the first phase of deployment of the EIC, which was carried out in Italy during 2001, 100.000 ID cards manufactured and initialized by the italian mint (IPZS), were assigned to 83 municipalities, in proportion to their respective population. Municipalities also received hardware and software tools needed for issuing ID cards to citizens, and have been given the opportunity of obtaining support by different means, including on site assistance, through a call center, and by accessing a dedicated Internet site.

The feedback received from the organizations involved in the experimental phase represents an invaluable contribution to the success of the project, as no experience was available with projects having similar characteristics in terms of geographic distribution, inter-organizational issues and sensitivity of data, even in other countries.

The experience gained during this experimental phase, helped in identifying the activities which must be carried out by the organizations involved, as well as technical and organizational requirements needed for guaranteeing correct operation of the overall architecture.

The second phase of deployment of the Italian EIC architecture has already started. The target of this second phase is to provide the 56 municipalities involved with 1.500.000 EICs, and to issue them by the end of year 2004 thus satisfying the local demand for ID cards. 400.000 EICs have been issued to citizens by the end of October 2004.

The overall financial effort sustained by the italian government for all the various design, testing and experimentation phases has been, up to the end of 2004, about 70 millions Euros.

We recall that, by Italian laws, municipalities are the only organizations which are responsible for issuing EICs to citizens. In particular, they form personal and biometric data to be written on the EIC and subsequently activate the EIC itself. However, in order to complete the process of issuing an EIC, several activities must be performed by other institutional organizations, possibly by interacting with municipalities.

The main activities performed during the deployment of the EIC architecture and during the issue of the EIC are described below.

Fiscal code coherence. This activity is performed in order to establish coherence between data held by Personal Data Registries at municipalities, which contain essential data needed for issuing identity cards, and data owned by the Ministry of Finance, which is the unique responsible for releasing fiscal codes to citizens. Ensuring validity of a citizen's fiscal code is especially important as, by law [Law63], it must be used in all communications with PAs for univocally identifying a fiscal subject.

INA setup and operation. This activity involves the creation and the management of a central archive, located at the Ministry of Interior, containing synthetic information about the relationship between citizens' personal data and the municipalities which are responsible for managing citizens' data. The INA archive is consulted by various organizations during the emission of an EIC for certifying the correctness and the validity of personal data to be written on it. The INA architecture is described in detail in Section 3.

Manufacturing and initialization of EIC. The Italian mint, IPZS, manufactures EICs by assembling its components and initializes them by setting up the microchip and the laser band. Moreover, IPZS initializes each card by writing on it a nation-wide unique code, provided by the Ministry of Interior. Municipalities perform requests to IPZS for lots of "blank" EICs. IPZS, upon receiving such formal offline request, contacts the SSCE for an authorization decision. Only after successful approval of the request by SSCE, IPZS delivers EICs to the requesting municipality.

Appliances setup at municipalities. During this activity, municipalities are equipped with special purpose hardware and software appliances which are needed for issuing EICs to citizens and for ensuring security in communication with interacting parties.

Personal and biometric data acquisition. Municipalities can acquire citizens' personal data either by using a web-based application or by standard offline procedures performed at the municipalities' offices. In both cases, information supplied by the requesting citizen is checked for validity against INA's data.

In case of acquisition of personal data via a web-based application, the municipality's system verifies coherence with personal data present in its database. If all validity checks are successful, the system makes a date with the citizen for completing the request at the municipality's offices. Otherwise, an error message is returned to the requesting subject.

Instead, biometric data, like photos and fingerprints, can only be acquired at the municipalities' offices.

Data formation and exchange. This activity involves secure data exchange between a municipality and SSCE, as well as formation of data to be written on the different parts of EICs (microchip, laser band and polycarbonate support) which are essential for enabling access to e-government services.

In particular, by using a special-purpose cryptographic software, municipalities generate for each EIC a certificate request in the PKCS#10 format containing personal and biometric data of the requesting citizen. Then the certificate request is sent to SSCE, which performs validity checks on the information provided, possibly by contacting other services, like INA for example. If all checks are successful, SSCE returns a certificate to the requesting municipality, signed with its private key. Of course, for reasons of efficiency, certificate requests can be sent in lots.

EIC release. Upon receipt of the certificate, the municipality is ready to release the EIC to the requesting citizen, along with a closed envelope containing a special sheet with the EIC keys printed on it, which are necessary for using the EIC for accessing digital government services and for revoking the EIC in case of theft.

Currently, there exist two procedures which can be used for issuing an EIC: (i) the "on-line" procedure, and (ii) the "off-line" procedure.

When following the "on-line" procedure, all activities required for issuing the EIC, except initialization, are performed "on line", while the citizen is waiting at the desk of the Personal Data Registry office of the municipality, as described above.

During the "off-line" procedure, some of the activities required for issuing EICs are performed by a third party, the Service Center (SC), which is typically an organization constituted by neighbor federated municipalities providing services in various fields to people living in the same region.

The Service Center is thus a new actor taking part in the issue of the EIC, as described below, with specific liabilities towards Municipalities and SSCE.

The SC receives from municipalities, personal and biometric data of citizens which requested the EIC, in univocally identified lots. Then, it performs a first validity check of personal data against INA. If this check is successful, the SC uses data provided by the municipality to generate a certificate request, performing the data formation and secure exchange activity described above. However, differently from what happens during the on-line procedure, SSCE returns a certificate whose status is "suspended". When the citizen goes back to the municipality's office for obtaining the EIC, the operator verifies that personal and biometric data on the EIC correspond to those of the requesting subject and, again, that it is coherent with INA's data. Then, if information on the card is valid, the operator changes the state of the certificate from "suspended" to "active"; at the same time the status of that EIC is set to "active" on the SSCE's database. Finally, the EIC is released to the citizen.

5.   The Security Backbone

On the Information Technology level, our approach is rather different from the standard ones in the same application field: in a layered description of our architecture we place security services in a layer, called *Security Backbone*, clearly distinguished both from the communication and the application ones.

That is, we do not deal with security functions within application, but consider them as infrastructure services, much in the same way communication services are nowadays considered: from the application viewpoint, in fact, details regarding how messages are transported along the communication network up to their destination are completely transparent. In the same way, applications in our architecture do not take care of the management of security functions, which are instead provided by an independent layer put on top of the layer providing communication services.

In fact, notwithstanding the work already done and still under development for a full deployment of secure functions within the lower communication layers (e.g. IPv6, DNSsec) the existing communication infrastructure of the Internet is largely lacking for what regards basic security functions. The wide availability of commercial products dealing with IT security, on the other side, is not enough to recover from this situation, since they either requires a deep knowledge of a complex technology (e.g. firewall configuration) or put the burden of dealing with security functions in the applications' modules.

Also, due to the critical nature of functions provided by security services, these cannot be set-up in a completely dynamic way, but have to be established only after some kind of agreement among involved organizations is formally in place. This aspect was a further motivation for our choice of putting security services in a layer fully independent from the application one.

The Security Backbone therefore contains the following functional subsystems: (i) confidentiality and integrity services, (ii) authorization service, (iii) authentication service, (iv) documentation subsystem, (v) access policy management, and (vi) quality of service monitoring.

We now give some detail on the functions executed by the subsystems in the Security Backbone and how they have been realized.

Confidentiality and integrity services.   Protection of exchanged messages against eavesdropping and guarantee of their integrity are provided through a mechanism resembling the behaviour of SSL/TSL. TCP packets are encrypted before transmission using symmetric cryptography based on session keys.

Authorization service.   This subsystem takes care of the initial set-up of functions in the security layer. A part of a Municipality's private key is distributed by CNSD to the Municipality itself by means of the internal registered mail of the Ministry of the Interior. On the basis of the part of the private key distributed by CNSD an exchange of encrypted messages between the local subsystem and a central control server happens, aiming at registering the local subsystem at the central control server. Hardware identifiers of the communicating machines are exchanged during this phase, so that it is possible to uniquely identify physical sites having the right to access the communication network.

Authentication service.   Guarantee of the identification of source and of destination of messages is implemented by having local and remote modules of the authentication subsystem exchange messages in a "tunneled" way. That is, an end-to-end communication tunnel is established having as its endpoints the local and the remote modules of the authentication subsystems: tunnel is implemented by encrypting TCP packets and placing them as the payload of IP packets addressed to the other endpoint of the tunnel.

Documentation subsystem. A dedicated subsystem of the Security Backbone [ACN+01c, AMN+02a, AMN+02b], has the task of recording all application-level messages exchanged between authorized access points of the communication network, so that documentation can be produced, if needed, on which data was actually exchanged. In fact, since communications related to personal data are often executed to discharge legal obligations, it is important the overall system is able to document, when a problem is later found, if and when communications where sent and received.

Access policy management. At CNSD site it is possible to define and enforce the desired policy for access management. In fact, both authorization and documentation services are fully parameterized, hence it is possible, from the central control point to implement various control policies for accesses to the system.

Quality of service monitoring. Since in the digital government service framework very often a legal value is attached to information exchanged, it is not possible to use, for quality of service measuring and monitoring, estimation based approaches.

For our purposes, in fact, we need to measure and to certify actual performance of service flows which spread in the network in consequence of an end-user's request [AFG+03, AFN+03].

Our solution to implement a secure distributed interoperability among Municipalities and PAs to provide secure digital government service in the field of Personal Data Registries is based on establishing a permanent infrastructure layer (the Security Backbone) providing security services, placed between the base communication services layer and the application service layer.

The single functional components we have used to build the Security Backbone are not, just by themselves, an intrinsic innovation, since each of them is already known in the literature. But their combination in setting up a permanent infrastructure layer providing security services is surely an innovation in the area of distributed e-services based on the interoperability of legacy systems.

In our vision, security functions in e-services have to be based on a permanent infrastructure layer, since this is the only approach able to guarantee, at a reasonable cost, efficiency of e-service provision and effectiveness of security in an open and intrinsically insecure environment like the Internet.

It is important to stress that in the real world of non-electronic services and whenever some kind of contractual responsibility is involved, security functions are always based, to various degree, on some form of permanent infrastructure. For example, public utilities like power supply, water, and sewage are provided by Municipalities to houses on the basis of the house ownership or renting. People interacts with banks in buildings and offices clearly and permanently identifiable as bank settings (even ATMs are usually placed in trustable environments). Also the currently most widespread e-service among the ones where trust is a fundamental aspect, that is e-banking, is based on an initial set-up phase where a security infrastructure is established: the person goes physically to branch offices to sign the contract and to receive codes and other eventual instructions to access the service on the Internet.

A further important point regarding security in interaction between institutions (as opposed to interaction among people) is that it is not generally accepted by organizations that any inside person can unilaterally establish trust to the outside. The reality of institutional cooperation shows that inter-institutional trust is always based on bilateral agreement at the organizational level. The electronic counterpart of this point is that, at the IT level, there must be an infrastructure layer providing security functions.

Note also that our architectural solution can be used independently from and simultaneously with local provisions in organizations to deal with security (e.g. perimeter firewalls, physical access control, personal identification, ...).

Also, advances in lower level protocols for communication (e.g. IPv6) or PKI-based approaches to interorganizational security infrastructures will hopefully result in a widespread intrinsically secure communication infrastructure. For the time being, though, relying on the availability of such technologies to provide secure services does not constitute a solution that in general works.

On the other side, the architecture we have described in this paper can be implemented with commercially available components and does not require updates or change to existing end-user applications. We therefore thinks it may contribute to spread further the use of digital government services for those areas where security is a primary concern.

6. Conclusions

In this paper we have described the deployment of a distributed digital government architecture dealing with the issue of Electronic Identity Cards in Italy.

We have presented a solution to the provision of security services which can be deployed without relying on advanced security technologies and without needing any update or change to existing systems and applications.

The various functional subsystems used in our solution, called the Security Backbone, provide end-to-end security in the interaction among involved organizations and constitutes an addition, not a replacement, of security solutions deployed locally.

The baseline of our approach is that security services have to be part of an infrastructure layer of inter-organizational communication, to be placed between the (lower) communication service layer and the (higher) application service layer. Only in this way is possible to provide at reasonable cost efficiency of service provision and effectiveness of security functions.

References

[ACN+99a] F.Arcieri, C.Cammino, E.Nardelli, M.Talamo, A.Venza: The Italian Cadastral Information System: a Real-Life Spatio-Temporal DBMS, *Workshop on Spatio-Temporal Database Management (STDBM'99)*, Edinburgh, Scotland, U.K., Sep.99, Lecture Notes in Computer Science vol.1678, 79–99, Springer-Verlag.

[ACM+01] F.Arcieri, E.Cappadozzi, G.Melideo, E.Nardelli, P.Naggar, M.Talamo: A formal model for data coherence maintenance. *Int. Workshop on Foundations of Models for Information Integration (FMII'01)*, 10th Workshop in the series Foundation of Models and Languages for Data and Objects (FMLDO), Viterbo, Italy, Sep.01. Lecture Notes in Computer Science Vol., Springer-Verlag. 2001.

[ACN+99b] F.Arcieri, E.Cappadozzi, P.Naggar, E.Nardelli, M.Talamo: Access Key Warehouse: a new approach to the development of cooperative information systems, *4th Int. Conf. on Cooperative Information Systems (CoopIS'99)*, Edinburgh, Scotland, U.K., 46–56, Sep.99.

[ACN+02] F.Arcieri, E.Cappadozzi, P.Naggar, E.Nardelli, M.Talamo: Coherence Maintainance in Cooperative Information Systems: the Access Key Warehouse Approach, *Int. J. of Cooperative Information Systems*, 11(1-2):175–200, 2002.

[ACN+01a] F.Arcieri, E.Cappadozzi, E.Nardelli, M.Talamo: Geographical information systems interoperability through distributed data exchange, *1st International Workshop on Databases, Documents, and Information Fusion (DBFusion'01)*, Magdeburg, Germany, May 01, Preprint n.8/2001, Fakultät für Informatik, Universität Magdeburg.

[ACN+01b] F.Arcieri, E.Cappadozzi, E.Nardelli, M.Talamo: Distributed territorial data management and exchange for public organizations, *3rd International Workshop on Advanced Issues of E-Commerce and Web-Based Information Systems (WECWIS'01)*, San Jose, Ca., USA, Jun.01, IEEE Computer Society Press, 2001.

[ACN+01c] F.Arcieri, E.Cappadozzi, E.Nardelli, M.Talamo: SIM: a working example of an e-government service infrastructure for mountain communities, *Workshop on Electronic Government (DEXA-eGov'01)*, Conf. on Databases and Expert System Applications (DEXA'01), Sep.01, Munich, Germany, IEEE Computer Society Press, 2001.

[AFG+03] F.Arcieri, F.Fioravanti, R. Giaccio, E.Nardelli, M.Talamo: Certifying performance of cooperative services in a digital government framework. *Int. Symposium on Applications and the Internet (SAINT-03)*, Orlando, Fl., USA, Jan.03, IEEE Computer Society Press, 2003.

[AFN+03] F.Arcieri, F.Fioravanti, E.Nardelli, M.Talamo: Inter-organizational E-Services Accounting Management. *3rd IFIP conference on e-Commerce, e-Business, and e-Government (I3E-03)*, Sao Paolo, Brasil, Sep.03, Kluwer Academic Publishers, 2003.

[AGN+01] F.Arcieri, R.Giaccio, E.Nardelli, M.Talamo: A framework for inter-organizational public administration network services. *Int. Conf. on Advances in Infrastructure for Electronic Business, Science, and Education on the Internet (SSGRR'01)*, L'Aquila, Italy, Aug.01. IEEE Computer Society Press, 2001.

[AMN⁺01] F.Arcieri, G.Melideo, E.Nardelli, M.Talamo: On the Dynamics of an Infrastructural Approach Supporting Coherence Maintenance for Inter-Organizational Collaboration, *Int. Symp. on Business Strategy Based Software Engineering (SoftwareTrends'01)*, Sept.01, Gersau, Switzerland, NetAcademy Press.

[AMN⁺02a] F.Arcieri, G.Melideo, E.Nardelli, M.Talamo: Experiences and issues in the realization of e-government services. *Int. Workshop on Research Issues in Data Engineering (RIDE'02)*, San Jose, Ca., USA, Feb.02. IEEE Computer Society Press, 2002.

[AMN⁺02b] F.Arcieri, G.Melideo, E.Nardelli, M.Talamo. A reference architecture for the certification of e-services in a digital government infrastructure. *Distributed and Parallel Databases*, 12:217–234, 2002.

[EIMI01] A.K.Elmagarmid, W.J.McIver: The Ongoing March Toward Digital Government, Guest Editors' Introduction to the special section on Digital Government, *IEEE Computer*, 34(2):32–38, Feb.01.

[JGA⁺01] J.Joshi, A.Ghafoor, W.G.Aref, E.H.Spafford: Digital Government Security Infrastructure Design Challenges. *IEEE Computer*, 34(2): 66-72, Feb.01.

[NTV99] E.Nardelli, M.Talamo, and P.Vocca. Efficient searching for multidimensional data made simple. *7th Annual European Symposium on Algorithms (ESA'99)*, Prague, Czech Republic, Jul.99, Lecture Notes in Computer Science vol.1643, pp. 339–353, Springer-Verlag.

[TCDE00] IEEE TCDE Bulletin, Special Issue on Data Cleaning, 23(4), Dec.2000.

[Law63] Law n.63, 17/mar/1993.

[Law1228] Law n.1228, 24/dec/1954.

[Law26] Law n.26 28/feb/2001.

[MD02] Ministerial Decree of 23/apr/2002 of the Ministry of Interior.

PROBLEMS RUNNING UNTRUSTED SERVICES AS JAVA THREADS

Almut Herzog
Dept. of Computer and Information Science
Linköping University, Sweden
almhe@ida.liu.se

Nahid Shahmehri
Dept. of Computer and Information Science
Linköping University, Sweden
nahsh@ida.liu.se

Abstract   A number of Java environments run untrusted services as Java threads. However, Java threads may not be suitably secure for this task because of its problem with safe termination, resource control and thread isolation. These problem areas have been recognised by the research community and are comprehensively addressed in the not yet implemented Java Isolate API. Meanwhile, Java threads continue to be used for running untrusted code.

This paper examines the risks associated with Java threads that run untrusted code and presents existing research solutions. Requirements for a secure execution environment are presented. The requirements are contrasted by recommendations and problems when using Java threads for running untrusted code.

Keywords: Java, server, security, thread, untrusted code, termination, requirements for a secure execution environment

1.   Introduction

There are a number of server environments or *containers* that run untrusted Java code: Applets in web browsers, servlets in web servers, Enterprise Java Beans (EJB) in their EJB containers, OSGi bundles in their framework—to name a few. In all the examples, the untrusted code must adhere to a certain API. In all scenarios the code comes from different sources and was developed without knowledge about other code that runs in the same container. Normally all named containers make use of Java threads to run the untrusted code.

In operating systems, protection between threads of the same process is usually low because the design idea of threads is that they are co-operative and friendly—they are meant to achieve a common goal. Whereas processes may originate from different users, and may be hostile to one another, only a single user is meant to own an individual task with multiple threads [SG97].

In Java containers, this is not necessarily so and Java designers have only lately built protection mechanisms that prevent one thread from modifying and specifically from stopping other threads [Oak01, OW99]. In Java 1.1, this was not done yet, and consequently threads could terminate other threads within the Java virtual machine. An attack applet demonstrated that it could destroy all other applets in a browser [LaD97]; but the vulnerability was also used to check which applets were currently executing in a browser and to kill unwanted applets [HT98].

But there is not only the problem of directly manipulating another thread. Untrusted code should be prevented by its container to starve other threads. For this, resource management is needed which is not currently provided by any Java implementation.

For some containers (e.g. the OSGi framework) it is important to reliably perform life cycle management of the untrusted code it runs. Life cycle management comprises stopping the untrusted code (called bundle), updating it with a new bundle uploaded by a provider and restarting it. If the bundle cannot be stopped in a timely fashion (or not at all) the life cycle management fails and at the worse leaves the container in a hung state that may also affect applications it runs.

This paper explores the suitability of Java threads for running untrusted code and points to earlier and on-going research that deals with problems encountered. We arrive at recommendations that should be considered when building a Java container that runs untrusted code as Java threads when using an existing Java Virtual Machine.

The paper is structured as follows. In section 2, we examine existing Java container problems and refer to attempts to their solution. Section 3 states requirements that a secure container should fulfill. Section 4 is the main part and shows how a technical implementation of the stated requirements are supported or thwarted by the current Java implementaton. Section 5 concludes the paper.

2.   Problems

The problem areas that are not well covered by Java threads are safe termination and resource control, and to a lesser extent also isolation. In the following sections we elaborate these problems and point to existing research solutions.

Safe Termination

In 2002, there was a rather inflamed debate in the Java newsgroups about running untrusted code as threads within a container. The discussion started with a message that complained that there was no recommended, safe way to stop a Java thread [Gal02]. The stop()-method within the Thread class is deprecated because it is not safe to use [Sun99, Hag99]. Consequently, there is no way to enforce that a thread terminates. Because of this, malicious threads can keep alive as long as they want. Their not-terminating may be enough to bring the execution environment into a hung state when it wants to shut down or uninstall the application to which this thread belongs (and waits indefinitely for the thread to terminate).

Example: An OSGi framework implementation (SGADK 3.1 (Service Gateway Application Developers' Kit) by Gatespace (www.gatespace.com), which is based on the OSGi specification 2.0) addresses the problem of termination by starting all threads created by bundles as daemon threads. A daemon thread is a thread that can be disregarded when the Java Virtual Machine wants to exit. It is meant to be used for helper threads like the garbage collector. This solution can simply be circumvented by a malicious thread by setting itself to be a non-daemon thread in its constructor:

```
public class MaliciousThread extends Thread {
    public MaliciousThread() {
        setDaemon(false);
    }
}
```

If a bundle in the used OSGi implementation specifically starts a non-daemon thread, the framework will hang on its shutdown command because it waits for the non-daemon thread to terminate (the System.exit()-method is not explicitly invoked). If that thread is looping or waiting forever, it effectively prevents the framework from shutting down and impairs its availability, because the framework is in a hung state.

Rudys and others [LPR99, RW02] have addressed safe thread termination by bytecode rewriting of every untrusted class. In the modified bytecode, it is checked at certain places in the code whether the code should terminate, much like the solution mandated by other literature [Sun99, Hag99]. The termination flag is checked on every backwards branch, at the beginning of every catch block and before every method call. However, it remains unclear if the solution can interrupt in a timely way a long-lasting native call such as writing a big chunk of a file over a slow network. The authors are aware that their solution encompasses a heavy performance penalty up to 100% and that they have not addressed the problem that an attacker could try to write code that explicitly attacks the rewriting algorithm.

Resource Control

Even though Java has good support for access control to resources through the Security Manager, once access is granted the resource is handed unrestrictedly to the client code. If for example the code in *malicious.jar* is allowed to write to /tmp/a, it may well fill the disk by writing an enormous amount of data to it. If *malicious.jar* is allowed to read certain files, it may well keep them open "for ever", thus effectively blocking them for other users or possibly reaching the operating system resource constraint of maximum number of open files per user or user process.

This lack of *release control* or *resource control* has been identified as a serious problem by the research community and solutions abound [CvE98, BCS01, BLT98, BHV01, CB02, CSN00, GL02, HS02, LP99, SBB⁺01] (see table 1 for a summary of resource-aware Java Virtual Machines). The most influential work is JRes, the resource-accounting interface for Java [CvE98]. The basic idea is to add resource accounting and limiting facilities to Java as a class library that replaces other core Java classes by bytecode rewriting. Due to a lack of resource management Java can neither prevent malicious code from using too many resources nor can it charge the code for the resources it is using. JRes is designed to address this problem. Both Web servers (running servlets) and Web browsers (running applets) are affected. JRes introduces a resource manager class that co-exists with the Java class loader and the security manager. The resource manager contains native code for CPU and memory accounting. Overuse callbacks are generated and throw exceptions when resource limits are exceeded. As JRes is not built into the JVM, there are a number of restrictions on what it can do. It specifically can not change the thread scheduling algorithm, take control of the scheduler or access the memory allocator and garbage collector. This work has eventually lead to the defintion of a resource management interface for the Java platform [CHS⁺03] that overcomes many shortcomings of JRes and may be incorporated into the Java platform in the future.

Isolation

Isolation among classes in the same runtime environment is achieved by the class loading mechanism [Gon98, LB98]. The Java class loader ensures that different implementations of classes with the same fully qualified name can exist in different class loaders. Apart from the name space advantage, the mechanism also prevents that a malicious class loader corrupts the classes used by another class loader by purposely loading a malicious class into that class loader's name space [JP00].

However, class loading is not a perfect isolation mechanism. Interference among classes that execute in the same Java virtual machine can still happen.

Name	Resources	Policy	Implementation
JRes [CvE98]	CPU, memory, network	Policy must be programmed as Java code but is otherwise versatile.	Use of the Java native interface (JNI) for CPU and memory accounting, bytecode rewriting.
– [BLT98]	CPU, memory	In a policy file with unknown syntax, permissions did not exist in Java 1.1	Based on a modified 1.1 Java virtual machine, mapping of Java threads to POSIX threads with realtime behaviour, modified Java heap manager allocates a fixed memory quota per protection domain.
Aroma [SBB$^+$01]	CPU, disk, network	The resource control mechanisms allow limits to be placed on the rate and quantity of resources used by Java threads. Syntax unknown.	Java virtual machine based on C++-classes using native threads, Java 1.2.2 compatible; four to 11 times slower than a Sun or IBM Java implementation.
SOMA [BCS01]	CPU, memory, (bandwidth, disk space)	Unknown. Support for the policy language Ponder [CML$^+$00] is future work.	Based on the Java VM Profiler Interface and JNI; bandwidth and disk space are not controlled only monitored.
Real-time Java www.rtj.org	CPU	Hard-coded	Choice of different thread schedulers that implement different policies.
– [LP99]	CPU	A language for the specification of resource limits is meant to be part of this work but a description is omitted due to lack of space	Based on a modified 1.1 Java virtual machine through modification of the thread scheduler.
Spout [CSN00]	CPU, memory	In a configuration file with unknown syntax.	Based on a modified 1.1 Java virtual machine. Resource accounting is updated for each method call. Little information is provided as resource control is only a side effect of Spout.
J-SEAL2 [BHV01]	CPU, memory, threads	In a Java object	Bytecode rewriting
JRAF [CB02]	CPU, memory, more resources may be plugged in	In an XML configuration file	Bytecode rewriting, a framework for resource accounting
Raje [GL02]	CPU, memory, sockets	Contract-based. The component comes with a policy.	Modified Kaffe JVM 1.0.6 with Linux C code
- [HS02]	Java-mediated resources	Extended Java policy file syntax.	Based on a modified 1.3 Java virtual machine. Uses the existing access controller to make resource control decisions.

Table 1. Resource-aware Java virtual machines

Czajkowski and Daynès [CD01] name the following remaining problems: Mutable parts of classes, typically static fields and static synchronised methods of system classes, can leak object references and can allow one application to prevent others from invoking certain methods. Internalised strings introduce shared, easy to capture monitors. Sharing event and finalisation queues can block or hinder the execution of some applications. Also, class loading is wasteful because of the code replication that is happening. Czajkowski says [Cza00]: "Typically, class loaders *do not share enough*: they replicate the code of application classes. Second, class loaders *share too much*: they share static fields of system classes."

Better isolation is achieved by the Multitasking Virtual Machine (MVM) [CD01] that particularly addresses the problem of executing different applications in the same Java virtual machine. MVM is a modified Java HotSpot virtual machine that shares application code wherever possible and replicates code where that is needed. In addition, native libraries, usually forbidden in safe Java environments, are contained by running them in a different process [CDW01] than the MVM.

MVM is closely related to the new Isolate API [JSR01, PCDV02]. An isolate is "a handle to an isolated computation" and allows controlled handling of that computation such as starting, suspending, resuming, and terminating. This safe life-cycle management is achieved by a strict isolation of the tasks and duplication of shared classes. The Isolate API is proposed but any implementation is currently dormant [Sop].

3.   Requirements for a Secure Container

In previous work [Her02, HS04b], we have defined a secure container as an environment built in such a way that an application cannot harm other applications within the container, the container itself, the underlying operating system, hardware or connected network nodes. The more elaborate requirements are the following.

1 An application shall not use local or connected resources (CPU, RAM, temporary disk, bandwidth, etc.) in such a way that it would prevent other software from executing.

2 An application shall not explore or modify the local node (other applications, the container, the operating system, hardware) unless authorised.

3 An application shall not explore or modify connected nodes (local or remote) unless authorised.

The implementation of a Java container that enforces these requirements using vanilla Java threads to run the application is not possible with the current Java implemententation, partly due to isolation problems among Java threads

No.	Requirement	Recommendations and caveats
1	An application shall not use local or connected resources (CPU, RAM, temporary disk, bandwidth, etc.) in such a way that it would prevent other software from executing.	Thwarted by *unsafe thread termination*, *insufficient isolation* and *lack of resource control*.
2	An application shall not explore or modify the local node (other applications, the container, the operating system, hardware) unless authorised.	Addressed by the security manager's *existing access control* but possibly thwarted by *default policy*, *default thread security*, *coarse-grained thread access*, and *stepping out of the sandbox*.
3	An application shall not explore or modify connected nodes (local or remote) unless authorised.	Solved partially by the security manager's *existing access control* but only socket based network access is subject to access control.

Table 2. Requirements for a secure execution environment and existing recommendations and caveats. Refer to the items listed in section 4 for more details on the keywords in italics.

and partly because of the missing resource control features. In the following section, we put up recommendations and caveats that should be considered by container designers.

4.   Recommendations and Caveats

Having described a number of problems that occur when multiple, untrusted applications execute in the same Java virtual machine, this section contains recommendations that should be considered by container designers in the absence of existing, reliable solutions. The recommendations show the current limits of Java but also how to efficiently use existing security features. For each recommendation or caveat we state which of the above requirements it solves or thwarts (see table 2 for a summary).

There is a technical and non-technical solution. The non-technical solution consists of a contract between container and application.

- *Contract* (solves the requirements but does not enforce them) EJB containers for example have a contract with the Enterprise JavaBeans that they execute. The contract is mandated by the Enterprise JavaBeans specification (see *Chapter 25: Runtime Environment* of the specification [Suna]). The beans are restricted in many ways (they must not start threads, must not use I/O, etc.) but the beans can get access to that functionality through the container. It is then up to the container to manage security aspects, e.g. to safely stop a thread or manage I/O. There is no enforcement of that contract, but the bean that violates it is not compliant and may not run in compliant containers. Such a contract may be useful for other containers as well.

A technical solution is difficult because of the earlier mentioned shortcomings of the existing Java Virtual Machine. There is no perfect way for running untrusted code as Java threads yet but the following recommendations give insight in problematic areas and address possible solutions, extensions or work-arounds.

- *Unsafe thread termination* (thwarts requirement 1) Container designers need to be aware that there is no guaranteed way to stop threads unless the Java virtual machine exits, too. Only the java.lang.System.exit()-method will effectively terminate all running threads, regardless of their state. Any clean-up is then done by the operating system as a result of the death of the Java virtual machine process.

  If the container needs to stop threads and needs to rely on the fact that the thread actually stops, then this is not possible in a safe way in Java (and probably all other thread APIs). The reason for this is that threads do not keep track of their resources, which is one of their distinctions from heavyweight processes. With processes, the operating system can perform the clean-up because there is information about process states.

  Consequently, if reliably stopping threads is an issue for the container, one should consider running the untrusted code as a separate process in its own Java virtual machine (until the Isolate API has been implemented). This achieves good isolation from other processes and allows resource control on the operating system level. Applications are still able to communicate with each other—Java has support for inter-process communication through the java.lang.Runtime and java.lang.Process classes and through sockets. On the other hand, separate processes imply a great memory and startup overhead because of the many replications of the runtime environment and maybe also application classes.

  A research solution by Rudys and others [LPR99, RW02] addresses safe thread termination (see section 2.1).

- *Insufficient isolation* (thwarts requirement 1) Different applications are usually loaded by different class loaders into the runtime environment. However, class loaders do not offer perfect isolation between applications. System classes are still shared. A malicious application may use access to system classes to stage denial-of-service attacks for other applications. It may e.g. hijack the finaliser queue (which is shared), it may explicitly or implicitly invoke the garbage collector (which suspends all other threads while it runs), it may monopolise the standard input and standard output stream, etc. This is addressed by the Isolate API [JSR01, PCDV02].

- *Lack of resource control* (thwarts requirement 1) Access to the CPU should be controlled, so that one application cannot starve other applications. This is possible with resource-aware Java virtual machines as mentioned in section 2.2 or by running each application in its own virtual machine and operating process.

- *Existing access control* (solves requirements 2 and 3) What resources application threads are allowed to access can be regulated with Java's security manager. The security manager should be activated by default, and the default policy for applications should be restrictive. By carefully tuning garbage collection and certain reordering of permissions in the policy file, the performance of a Java virtual machine with a security manager is usually acceptable [HS04a].

- *Default policy* (complicates requirement 2) The system default policy, hidden in the Java virtual machine installation directory, should be revised and probably overruled by a more rigid policy file for the execution environment. For instance, Sun's Java implementation comes with a system default policy that allows any thread to stop other threads.

- *Default thread security* (complicates requirement 2) Java's default security manager offers little protection for user threads from other threads. Any thread in the Java virtual machine can find any other non-system thread. Threads cannot stop arbitrary threads, but they can call the interrupt()-method of non-system threads. This can result in arbitrary behaviour because the interrupt()-method behaves differently depending on the state of the interrupted thread. The interrupt()-method is meant to signal to the executing thread that it should terminate. Thus, applications that correctly and politely respond to an interrupt can be shut down by a malicious application.

Also, in the standard security manager, the permission to modify a thread is only checked if the thread to be modified or stopped belongs to the system thread group. Consequently, the Java virtual machine protects itself and its system threads, but does not offer the same access control for application threads. Any application thread, although run under a standard security manager, can still find out about all threads in the Java virtual machine, except for threads in the system group. The motivation for this behaviour is unclear. The Java documentation [Sunb] is aware of this and suggests the implementation of a proprietary security manager that implements a stricter access control if that is needed by the application.

The container should use a security manager that implements access control for all threads and not only for system threads. Different policies for such access control are discussed e.g. in the section *Implementing Thread Security* of [Oak01].

- *Coarse-grained thread access* (complicates requirement 2) A more fine-grained policy for thread access may be needed, because a permission is granted for all threads or for no threads. A granularity of thread group may be more appropriate. For instances, it may be perfectly fine for a thread to manipulate other threads within its own group; at worst, it causes disarray among its own threads. However, manipulating threads outside the thread group of that application, especially system threads, is much more critical because this manipulation potentially affects other applications and the container.

- *Stepping out of the sandbox* (complicates requirement 2) Containers need to be careful that the code they run does not have permission to step out of its contained environment. A complete listing of all permissions and their implications can be found at [Sunc]. If the execution environment is meant to decide if it allows code that needs certain permissions, then knowledge about permission implications are vital. Also the contract between Enterprise JavaBeans and their containers [Suna] is a useful starting point for a reasonable default policy in a Java server environment. Some examples:

  - No application should be given permission to exit the Java virtual machine. That would effectively kill both the current thread and any other Java thread within the Java virtual machine as well as the operating system process of the Java virtual machine.

  - An application that comes with RuntimePermissions modifyThread, modifyThreadGroup or stopThread should be considered as potentially malicious. This application has the ability to manipulate all threads within the Java virtual machine including the threads that make up the execution environment and the Java virtual machine. Unfortunately, these permissions are required for code that uses RMI (remote method invocation).

  - No untrusted application should have permission to run native code in the same operating system process as the container. Native code executes outside the control of the Java security manager and interacts directly with the operating system. Native code is only restricted by limitations implemented by the operating system.

From these recommendations and the problems mentioned in section 2 it becomes clear that Java threads (as of J2SDK 1.5) are not suitable for running untrusted code. The only currently available resort is to use processes or to build on research prototypes. None of the three alternatives is attractive. For the time being, a solution based on a contract between the untrusted application and the container may be most suitable. However, a contract is not at all appropriate if the container executes completely unknown code such as applets in a web browser. In environments where more trust can be put on the application, where the origin of the application is known (as in JavaBeans, servlets and OSGi bundles) a contract solution may be an interim solution until the Isolate API is implemented.

5. Conclusion

To summarise, the Java thread model is currently not suitable for running untrusted code as threads. Operating system processes offer better isolation but with the obvious drawbacks of startup overhead, high memory consumption and heavyweight communication between applications. If threads must be used, the Java security manager enhanced with stronger thread control can control initial access to resources. A resource-aware Java virtual machine ensures that untrusted code does not hog CPU or memory. However, there is currently no support for isolation of threads from each other or a method for safely terminating a thread.

Research solutions exist and have even made it into a Java Community Process with the goal to introduce the Isolate API. This API will solve the shortcomings discussed in this paper. For the time being, a non-technical solution based on a contract between application and container may be most feasible.

References

[Gal02] <galaygalay@hotmail.com>. Sun's thread retardedness. http://comp.lang.java.programmer (visited 7-Apr-2004), 4-Apr-2002.

[BCS01] Paolo Bellavista, Antonio Corradi, and Cesare Stefanelli. How to monitor and control resource usage in mobile agent systems. In *Proceedings of the 3rd International Symposium on Distributed Objects and Applications (DOA '01)*, pages 65–75. IEEE, 2001.

[BHV01] Walter Binder, Jarle G. Hulaas, and Alex Villazón. Portable resource control in Java: The J-SEAL2 approach. In *Proceedings of the ACM Conference on Object-Oriented Programming, Systems, Languages, and Applications (OOPSLA '01)*, pages 139–155. ACM Press, October 2001.

[BLT98] Philippe Bernadat, Dan Lambright, and Franco Travostino. Towards a resource-safe Java for service guarantees in uncooperative environments. In *Proceedings of the IEEE Workshop on Programming Languages for Real-Time Industrial Applications*. IEEE, December 1998.

[CB02]   Vladimir Calderon and Walter Binder. JRAF–the Java resource accounting facil-
             ity. In *Proceedings of the Workshop on Resource Managment for Safe Languages
             (ECOOP'02)*. http://www.ovmj.org/workshops/resman/ (visited 22-Apr-
             2004), June 2002.

[CD01]   Grzegorz Czajkowski and Laurent Daynès. Multitasking without compromise:
             a virtual machine evolution. In *Proceedings of the ACM Conference on Object-
             Oriented Programming, Systems, Languages, and Applications (OOPSLA'01)*,
             pages 125–138. ACM Press, 2001.

[CDW01]   Grzegorz Czajkowski, Laurent Daynès, and Mario Wolczko. Automated and
             portable native code isolation. In *Proceedings of the 12th International Sym-
             posium on Software Reliability Engineering (ISSRE'01)*, pages 298–307. IEEE,
             2001.

[CHS+03]   Grzegorz Czajkowski, Stephen Hahn, Glenn Skinner, Pete Soper, and Ciaran
             Bryce. A resource management interface for the Java platform. Technical Report
             TR-2003-124, Sun Microsystems Laboratories, May 2003.

[CML+00]   Antonio Corradi, Rebecca Montanari, Emil Lupu, Morris Sloman, and Cesare
             Stefanelli. A flexible access control service for Java mobile code. In *Proceedings
             of the 16th Annual Conference on Computer Security Applications (ACSAC'00)*,
             pages 356–365. IEE, December 2000.

[CSN00]   Tzicker Chiueh, Harish Sankaran, and Anindya Neogi. Spout: A transparent
             distributed execution engine for Java applets. In *Proceedings of the IEEE In-
             ternational Conference on Distributed Computing Systems (ICDCS'00)*, pages
             394–401. IEEE, April 2000.

[CvE98]   Grzegorz Czajkowski and Thorsten von Eicken. JRes: A resource accounting
             interface for Java. In *Proceedings of the ACM Conference on Object-Oriented
             Programming, Systems, Languages, and Applications (OOPSLA'98)*, pages 21–
             35. ACM Press, October 1998.

[Cza00]   Grzegorz Czajkowski. Application isolation in the JavaŹ virtual machine. In
             *Proceedings of the ACM Conference on Object-Oriented Programming, Systems,
             Languages, and Applications (OOPSLA'00)*, pages 354–366. ACM Press, Octo-
             ber 2000.

[GL02]   Frédéric Guidec and Nicolas LeSommer. Towards resource consumption ac-
             counting and control in Java: a practical experience. In *Proceedings of the
             Workshop on Resource Managment for Safe Languages (ECOOP'02)*. http:
             //www.ovmj.org/workshops/resman/ (visited 22-Apr-2004), June 2002.

[Gon98]   Li Gong. Secure Java class loading. *IEEE Internet Computing*, 2(6):56–61,
             November 1998.

[Hag99]   Peter Haggar. *Practical Java—Programming Language Guide*. Addison Wesley,
             1999.

[Her02]   Almut Herzog. Secure execution environment for Java electronic services. Li-
             centiate Thesis No. 991. Linköping University, Sweden. http://www.ida.
             liu.se/~almhe/publications/tek-lic-991.pdf (visited 23-Apr-2004),
             December 2002.

[HS02]   Almut Herzog and Nahid Shahmehri. Using the Java sandbox for resource con-
             trol. In *Proceedings of the 7th Nordic Workshop on Secure IT Systems (Nord-
             Sec'02)*, pages 135–147. Karlstad University, November 2002.

[HS04a]   Almut Herzog and Nahid Shahmehri. Performance of the Java security manager. Submitted for publication, 2004.

[HS04b]   Almut Herzog and Nahid Shahmehri. Requirements for a secure Java application container. Submitted for publication, 2004.

[HT98]   Vesna Hassler and Oliver Then. Controlling applets' behavior in a browser. In *Proceedings of the 14th Annual Conference on Computer Security Applications (ACSAC'98)*, pages 120–125. IEEE, 1998.

[JSR01]   Java Community Process. JSR 121: Application isolation API specification. http://jcp.org/en/jsr/detail?id=121 (visited 22-Apr-2004).

[JP00]   Jamie Jaworski and Paul J. Perrone. *Java Security Handbook*. Sams Publishing, November 2000.

[LaD97]   Mark D. LaDue. Java insecurity. *Computer Security Journal*, 13(1):63–68, 1997.

[LB98]   Sheng Liang and Gilad Bracha. Dynamic class loading in the Java virtual machine. In *Proceedings of the ACM Conference on Object-Oriented Programming, Systems, Languages, and Applications (OOPSLA '98)*, pages 36–44. ACM Press, October 1998.

[LP99]   Manoj Lal and Raju Pandey. CPU resource control for mobile programs. In *Proceedings of the 3rd International Symposium on Mobile Agents*, pages 74–88. IEEE, 1999.

[LPR99]   Jiangchun Frank Luo, Liwei Peng, and Algis Rudys. Safe termination of Java classes. Project report, Dept. of Computer Science, Rice University, Houston, TX, November 1999.

[Oak01]   Scott Oaks. *Java Security*. O'Reilly & Associates, Inc., 2nd edition, 2001.

[OW99]   Scott Oaks and Henry Wong. *Java Threads*. O'Reilly & Associates, Inc., 2nd edition, 1999.

[PCDV02]   Krzysztof Palacz, Grzegorz Czajkowski, Laurent Daynès, and Jan Vitek. Incommunicado: Efficient communication for isolates. In *Proceedings of the 17th ACM Conference on Object-Oriented Programming, Systems, Languages, and Applications (OOPSLA'02)*, pages 262–274. ACM Press, November 2002.

[RW02]   Algis Rudys and Dan S. Wallach. Termination in language-based systems. *ACM Transactions on Information and System Security (TISSEC)*, 5(2):138–168, May 2002.

[SBB+01]   Niranjan Suri, Jeffrey M. Bradshaw, Maggie R. Breedy, Kenneth M. Ford, Paul T. Groth, Gregory A. Hill, and Raul Saavedra. State capture and resource control for Java: The design and implementation of the aroma virtual mach. In *Proceedings of the JavaŽ Virtual Machine Research and Technology Symposium*. Usenix, April 2001.

[SG97]   Avi Silberschatz and Peter Galvin. *Operating System Concepts*. Addison Wesley, 1997.

[Sop]   Pete Soper. [Isolate-interest] JSR 121 status? http://altair.cs.oswego.edu/pipermail/isolate-interest/2004-March/00009%9.html (visited 22-Apr-2004).

[Suna]   Sun Microsystems, Inc. Enterprise JavaBeans specification 2.1. http://java.sun.com/products/ejb/docs.html (visited 16-Apr-2004).

[Sunb]   Sun Microsystems, Inc. Java 2 platform, standard edition, v.1.5.0 API specifica-
              tion. `http://java.sun.com/j2se/1.5.0/docs/api/index.html` (visited
              7-Apr-2004).

[Sunc]   Sun Microsystems, Inc.   Permissions in the Java 2 SDK.   `http://java.`
              `sun.com/j2se/1.5.0/docs/guide/security/permissions.html` (visited
              15-Apr-2004).

[Sun99]   Sun Microsystems, Inc. Why are Thread.stop, Thread.suspend, Thread.resume
              and Runtime.runFinalizersOnExit deprecated. `http://java.sun.com/j2se/`
              `1.4.2/docs/guide/misc/threadPrimitiveDeprecati%on.html` (visited
              7-Apr-2004), 1999.

GENERATING NETWORK SECURITY PROTOCOL IMPLEMENTATIONS FROM FORMAL SPECIFICATIONS

Benjamin Tobler
Department of Computer Science, University of Cape Town
Private Bag, Rondebosh 7701, South Africa
btobler@cs.uct.ac.za

Andrew C.M. Hutchison
Department of Computer Science, University of Cape Town
Private Bag, Rondebosch 7701, South Africa
hutch@cs.uct.ac.za

Abstract   We describe the Spi2Java code generation tool, which we have developed in an attempt to bridge the gap between formal security protocol specification and executable implementation. Implemented in Prolog, Spi2Java can input a formal security protocol specification in a variation of the Spi Calculus, and generate a Java code implementation of that protocol. We give a brief overview of the role of code generation in the wider context of security protocol development. We cover the design and implementation of Spi2Java which we relate to the high integrity code generation requirements identified by Whalen and Heimdahl. By defining a Security Protocol Implementation API that abstracts cryptographic and network communication functionality we show that protocol logic code can be separated from underlying cryptographic algorithm and network stack implementation concerns. The design of this API is discussed, particularly its support for pluggable implementation providers. Spi2Java's functionality is demonstrated by way of example: we specify the Needham-Schroeder Public Key Authentication Protocol, and Lowe's attack on it, in the Spi Calculus and examine a successful attack run using Spi2Java generated implementation of the protocol roles.

Keywords: Code generation, Formal methods, Java, Process algebra, Prolog, Security, Spi Calculus

Introduction

Formal methods have been widely and successfully used to specify network security protocols and analyse their security properties to ensure correctness [MBN96, LGY90, Low95, AG98, THG99]. The same emphasis has, however, not been placed on the correctness of concrete implementations of these security protocol specifications. This is evident when one considers the number of security alerts issued for implementations of various security protocols. Flaws have been discovered in many software vendors' SSL implementations in the last year alone, including, but not limited to companies such as Apple, SCO, Microsoft, Cisco, and RSA and open source organizations OpenSSL, KDE and Apache [CERa, CERc, KDE, CERb]. It is clear then that security protocol research has been successful in verifying specifications, but that errors can still be introduced during implementation, leaving a gap between specification (formal and otherwise) and implementation.

In this paper we examine an approach to bridging this gap, by means of automatic code generation, in a manner that complements and integrates with the already existing formal methodologies for security protocol analysis.

Our approach entails the specification of a security protocol, in a variation of the Spi Calculus, which is used as input into our Spi2Java code generation tool. Spi2Java compiles the specification down to Java code that is a concrete implementation of the protocol.

Choosing the Spi Calculus as a specification language provides the benefits of formal specification: it allows the security protocol to be subject to analysis to ensure the desired security properties (i.e. one or more of *authenticity, confidentiality* and *integrity*) hold. Its formally defined semantics also provide a precise definition of the expected behaviour of the protocol, and so facilitates code generation and verification. These properties are particularly useful in helping to meet some of Whalen and Heimdahl's requirements for high-integrity code generation identified in [WH99].

Regarding related work, we are aware of some other projects in this area: one on generating code from CAPSL specifications [MM01], COSP-J [Did], AVGI [DXSP01] and another tool also called Spi2Java (which only came to our attention after the initial draft of this paper). COSP-J is based to some extent on Casper, a tool for converting fairly abstract security protocol specifications to CSP specifications, and produces Java code that implements protocols. Perrig et. al. briefly describe a tool for automatic security protocol implementation as part of AVGI in [DXSP01], however we have not been able to find further details of this tool in any available publications. Durante et. al. describe their own Spi2Java tool in [DPD04]. They do not address the issue of the correctness of the generated code wrt Spi, nor do they discuss the implementation of the tool itself, i.e. how the translation from Spi to Java is performed. We have, as yet, not found any published work detailing verification or proof of correctness of automatically generated code that implements security protocols.

Though there is some overlap with these projects, we believe aspects of our Spi2Java tool and our continuing work on it, make some contribution to the area of code generation for automatic security protocols implementation. We use the Spi Calculus as input, allowing our Spi2Java to complement verification tools, such as the MMC model checker for the π and Spi Calculi [PYS03]. Though abstraction of security functionality, e.g. Java's Cryptographic Extensions, is definitely not novel, our clean and complete separation of generated protocol logic code from cryptographic and network implementation specifics via an API provides even greater flexibility to the protocol implementor. Finally our continuing work towards meeting the requirements of high integrity code generation, specifically proving that our mapping from Spi to Java code segments preserves the Spi semantics in the Java code, will hopefully provide a high level of confidence in the correctness of the protocol logic implementation.

The layout of this paper is as follows: An overview of the security protocol development process is given indicating the role of a formal specification language throughout the process and emphasising the implementation and implementation verification phases of the process, where code generation can be used. We argue for the suitability of the Spi Calculus in the role of specification language, and define a variation of it to facilitate code generation. We cover the separation of protocol logic implementation from cryptographic algorithm and network communication implementation, by abstraction using the SPP API and the resulting benefits of this. We also define a mapping from Spi Calculus constructs to Java code segments and describe the code generation tool we have developed in Prolog that defines rules for these mappings. We look at verification of the tool and the generated code as well as current work validating the mappings from Spi Calculus constructs to Java code. Finally, we conclude the paper by assessing the contribution of this approach to bridging the gap between security protocol specification and implementation.

1. Security Protocol Development

Given that developing protocols to provide network security is a specialisation of software development in general, a security protocol development process could be described as follows (see Figure 1):

Requirements: Like any system, there may be requirements unrelated to security. However the requirements of interest in this paper are the desired security properties of the protocol - authentication, confidentiality and integrity. For brevity we view these requirements as input to the development process as opposed to a phase.

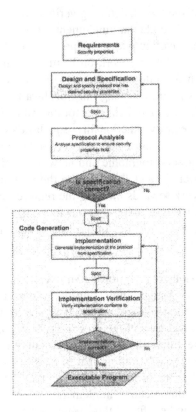

Figure 1.   Security protocol development process.

Design and Specification: A protocol that attempts to meet the requirements is designed and specified. The number of messages exchanged, message
contents and the cryptographic mechanisms employed will all depend on the
security properties stated in the requirements.

Protocol Specification Analysis: The protocol specification is analyzed, potentially by means of inference logics, e.g. BAN [MBN96] and
GNY [LGY90] and attack analysis techniques, e.g. strand-space analysis [THG99] and model checking [Low96, Den00] to determine whether the
required security properties hold. If not, the analysis results are fed back to
the design and specification phase and the protocol is modified or redesigned.
Otherwise the process can progress to the implementation phase.

Implementation: The protocol is implemented by, either manually or automatically, generating code that can be compiled to an executable program that
conforms to the specification.

Implementation Verification: Two approaches can be taken to ensure the correctness of the concrete implementation. In both cases the ideal is to be able to prove that the generated code is a refinement of the security protocol specification. Either the generated code for each protocol must be verified to ensure equivalence to the specification, or the translation process must be proven correct and the mappings from specification language constructs to implementation code must shown to preserve the specification language semantics [WH99].

This paper is concerned mainly with the last two phases: implementation and implementation verification, as indicated in the boxed area of Figure 1. These phases produce the output of the development process: an executable program that conforms to the security protocol specification for which the desired security properties hold.

Obviously it is desirable, and convenient, to be able to generate a protocol implementation from a specification defined in the same language used for analysing the correctness of the specification. This avoids the possibility of protocol semantics being lost in the translation from one specification language to another, and helps preserve them during the implementation phase. To that end we have selected the Spi Calculus to use as input for our code generator.

2. The Spi Calculus

The Spi Calculus, defined by Abadi and Gordon in [AG98], consists of a number of terms, such as names, variables, encrypted terms and pairs, and some simple processes which incorporate actions that include sending and receiving messages, decryption, term matching and parallel composition. Each of the processes has a simple, well defined behaviour. Despite it small size and relative simplicity, the Spi Calculus (and the π-calculus it is based on) is powerful in its ability to both describe, and reason about, the behaviour of concurrent systems [MPW92] - of which security protocols are a special case.

The behaviour of the processes of the π-calculus is defined formally by transition semantics in [MPW92]. These semantics are extended in [AG98] to define the behaviour of constructs that the Spi-Calculus introduces to model cryptographic operations such as symmetric and asymmetric encryption and message digests. These formal definitions provide a basis for reasoning about the security properties of protocols specified in the Spi Calculus as demonstrated in [AG98]. As formal specifications describe the expected behaviour of a protocol explicitly, they also provide a superior guide for the implementor, whether automated or human.

In the context of program refinement, as described by Morgan in [Mor98], Spi fulfills the roles of specification - it is high level abstraction that facilitates understanding - and to some extent code - executable instructions generally in an imperative language. Spi provides an abstraction that allows security protocols to be easily understood. It also serves as code in the sense that it defines executable behaviour for all its processes, as unlike the π-calculus it is based on, Spi does not define the non-executable binary summation process that specifies that a process P can behave as either process Q or R arbitrarily. In this context Spi2Java is essentially a compiler for the Spi Calculus.

Variation for Code Generation

To facilitate code generation we define a few variations to the standard Spi Calculus. Firstly, some minor syntactic changes are defined to allow security protocols to be described in plain text files. These include using the *!* and *?* characters to indicate output and input respectively - as in Occam [SGS95]. We also introduce the terms $pub(x)$ and $priv(x)$, which evaluate to the public and private keys of the principal x respectively, following an element of the syntax used by the Security Protocol Language described in [Cra03]. A process that checks the validity of a timestamp is also defined.

Secondly, only a subset, albeit a comprehensive one, of the terms and processes defined by the original calculus are supported: the successor term and integer case and replication processes are not supported.

Syntax and Semantics

A brief description of the syntax of the Spi Calculus variant and an informal description of the behaviour of its processes is given below for convenience. Apart from the variations we have defined, the following is just a summary of the description in [AG98], which also contains the formal definition of the language.

An infinite set of *names* and an infinite set of *variables* over those names are assumed. Names range over principal identifiers, nonces, keys and other values. Letting c, m, n, p and r range over names and x, y and z over variables, the terms are defined by the grammar:

$L, M, N ::=$

n	a name
(M, N)	a pair
x	a variable
$\{M\}N$	encryption of M with N
$hash(M)$	hash of M
$pub(n)$	public key of n
$priv(n)$	private key of n

and the processes by:

$P, Q ::=$

$$c!\langle N\rangle.P$$
$$c?(x).P$$
$$(P\,|\,Q)$$
$$(n)P$$
$$[M\ is\ N]P$$
$$nil$$
$$let\ (x,\ y)\ =\ M\ in\ P$$
$$case\ L\ of\ \{x\}N\ in\ P$$
$$case\ T\ valid\ in\ P$$

The behaviour of these processes is described informally as follows:

- $c!\langle N\rangle.P$ will output N on channel c when an interaction with an input process occurs, and then run as P.

- $c?(x).P$ will input a term, say N, on channel c when an interaction occurs and then run as $P[N/x]$ i.e. P with N substituted for all free occurrences of x.

- $(n)P$ creates a new, private name n and behaves like P. This process is used to model the generation of nonces.

- $[M\ is\ N]P$ behaves like P if the term M is the same as the term N or else it does nothing.

- nil does nothing.

- $let\ (x,\ y)\ =\ M\ in\ P$ allows M to be split. If M is a pair $(N,\ L)$ then $P[N/x][L/y]$ is run, otherwise the process does nothing.

- $case\ L\ of\ \{x\}N\ in\ P$ runs as $P[M/x]$ if M is L decrypted with with N, otherwise it does nothing.

- $case\ T\ valid\ in\ P$ runs as P if the timestamp T is valid otherwise does nothing.

To accommodate implementation, a preamble declaring variable types is specified. The supported types are *channel, encryption, hash, id, key, nonce, term* (generic or compound value) and *time*.

3.   Protocol Specification Example

As an example of protocol specification using the Spi Calculus we specify the Needham-Schroeder Public Key Authentication protocol. We first give the generally used standard notation version, which does not have formally defined semantics, and then a specification in Spi.

$$1 \quad A \rightarrow B : \{n, A\}pub(B)$$
$$2 \quad B \rightarrow A : \{n, m\}pub(A)$$
$$3 \quad A \rightarrow B : \{m\}pub(B)$$

This informal description, though simple and fairly intuitive, leaves the specification of most protocol actions implicit. The burden is on the protocol implementor to use her experience and understanding of security protocols, to determine the sequence of programmatic actions that implement this protocol correctly and with all of the designer's intended semantics. In particular, this example demonstrate the failure of the standard notation to explicitly specify when nonces should be instantiated and whether, and how, values in a received messages should be verified.

In contrast the Spi specification of the same protocol indicates exactly when nonces should be instantiated and which received values to verify and how.

The Spi specification defines a process for the initiator role in the protocol:

channel c *encryption* l
id A, B, y *nonce* m, n, x
term j

$Init(A, B, c) = (n)$
$\qquad c!\langle\{n, A\}pub(B)\rangle.$
$\qquad c?(l).$
$\qquad case\, l\, of\, \{j\}priv(A)\, in$
$\qquad let\, (x, m) = j\, in$
$\qquad [x\, is\, n]$
$\qquad c!\langle\{m\}pub(B)\rangle.$
$\qquad nil$

This process states explicitly when the initiator should generate the nonce n to challenge the responder, and how the first nonce in the message returned by the responder, indicated by the variable x, should be matched against it.

The responder process is specified as follows:

channel c *encryption* l, k
id B, x *nonce* m, n, y
term j

$Resp(B, c) = \quad c?(l).$
$\qquad case\, l\, of\, \{j\}priv(B)\, in$
$\qquad let\, (n, x) = j\, in$
$\qquad (m)$
$\qquad c!\langle\{(n, m)\}pub(x)\rangle.$

$$c?(k).$$
$$case\ k\ of\ \{y\}priv(B)\ in$$
$$[y\ is\ m]$$
$$nil$$

Like the initiator process, it also explicitly defines the generation of a challenge nonce and verification of the initiator's response to the challenge.

A run of the protocol is specified by the parallel execution of the initiator and responder processes:

$$channel\ c\quad id\ A,\ B$$

$$NSRun(A,\ B,\ c) =$$
$$(Init(A,\ B,\ c)\mid Resp(B,\ c))$$

where c is a channel allowing A and B to communicate.

Lowe's Attack on the Needham-Schroeder Protocol

Even if the implementation is faithful to the specification, an attacker can successfully masquerade as a legitimate participant in the Needham-Schroeder protocol, described by Lowe in [Low95], as follows:

1	A	$\to C:$	$\{n,\ A\}pub(C)$
2	$C(A)$	$\to B:$	$\{n,\ A\}pub(B)$
3	B	$\to C(A):$	$\{n,\ m\}pub(A)$
4	C	$\to A:$	$\{n,\ m\}pub(A)$
5	A	$\to C:$	$\{m\}pub(C)$
6	$C(A)$	$\to B:$	$\{m\}pub(B)$

where C is the attacker who leads B to erroneously believe that he is communicating with A, when in fact he is talking to C.

In Spi this attacker role is specified as follows:

$$channel\ cA,\ cB\quad encryption\ k,\ l,\ p$$
$$id\ A,\ B,\ C\quad\quad nonce\ m,\ n,\ x$$
$$term\ j$$

$$Attack(cA,\ cB,\ B,\ C) =$$
$$cA?(l).$$
$$case\ l\ of\ \{j\}priv(C)\ in$$
$$let\ (n,\ A) = j\ in$$
$$cB!\langle(n,\ A)pub(B)\rangle.$$
$$cB?(p).$$

$$cA!\langle p \rangle.$$
$$cA?(k).$$
$$case\, k\, of\, \{m\}priv(C)\, in$$
$$cB!\langle mpub(B) \rangle.$$
$$nil$$

and a run of successful attack can be specified by:

$$channel\, cAC,\, cBC \quad id\, A,\, B,\, C$$

$$NSRun(A,\, B,\, c) = \, Init(A,\, C,\, cAC)\,|$$
$$Attack(cAC,\, cBC,\, B,\, C)\,|$$
$$Resp(B,\, cBC)$$

where cAC is a channel for communication between A and C, and cBC is a channel for communication between C and B. The use of two separate channels allow the attacker to control communication between A and B at the network level. This approach models the Dolev-Yao attacker capabilities [DY81], where an attacker is able to intercept and remove messages sent by the legitimate protocol participants, as well as introduce new messages onto the network.

4.   The Spi2Java Code Generator

Rules Based Implementation

Spi2Java is implemented in Prolog using the Definite Clause Grammar rules supported by most Prolog engines [Wie03]. The third requirement identified by Whalen and Heimdahl for high integrity code generation is that *"Rigorous arguments must be provided to validate the translator and/or the generated code"* [WH99, Page 4]. Using Prolog does not in and of itself provide a proof of correctness of the translator software (Spi2Java) and hence meet this goal. However, given that in the development of Spi2Java the specification of the mapping from Spi to Java was essentially defined using Prolog rules, we can be confident (at least as much as our faith in the Prolog engine allows), that Spi2Java preserves those mappings. Whether or not the mappings preserve the semantics of Spi in the Java code is another matter, broached later in this paper.

It is important to note that formally verifying translator software is not, at least currently, a completely attainable goal. Doing so would require a verified programming language in which to implement the translator software, a verified compiler to compile the software to verifiable machine code, making calls to verified libraries, with a verified operating system, all running on a verified hardware architecture implementation [WH99, CHP90].

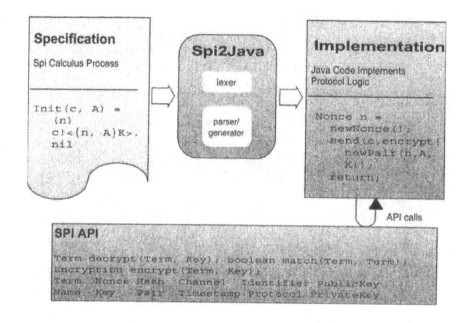

Figure 2. Code generation using Spi2Java.

The SPP API

In our approach we separate the implementation of the protocol logic from that of the cryptographic algorithms and network communications. We define:

Protocol Logic as the code that maintains protocol state, determines when and if messages are sent and received, the contents of outgoing messages, the expected contents of incoming messages, storing message components and and determining which incoming message components to verify and what components they should be verified against.

and

Cryptographic and Communications Provider: as provider specific code that handles the packing and unpacking of message components into byte streams, implements cryptographic algorithms (e.g. symmetric and asymmetric encryption and message digests) and manages network protocol specific aspects (e.g. message packing and unpacking, network addresses of principals and message transport).

Spi2Java generates code that implements the protocol logic. This code makes calls to the Security Protocol Primitives (SPP) API that abstracts the low level cryptographic and network communications details. The bridge de-

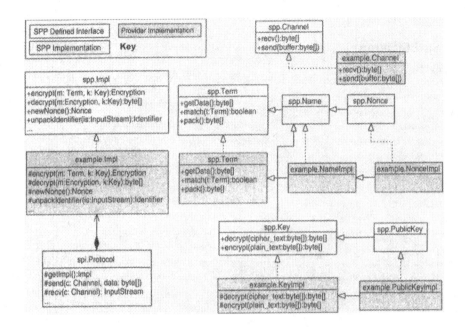

Figure 3.   UML class diagram of a subset of the SPP API.

sign pattern is employed here to decouple the provider specific cryptographic and communication implementation from the protocol logic code. SPP defines a set of interfaces for message components such as nonces, principal identifiers and keys as well as for cryptographic and communications operations (see Figure 3).

The abstract factory method design pattern is used allowing different providers to be plugged into the API. It gives the protocol logic code a single point of access to instances of the concrete provider classes that implement the SPP defined interfaces for value types and cryptographic and network operations. The flexibility of this approach means that providers can be changed without affecting the protocol logic code generated by Spi2Java. For example: a provider that implements RSA asymmetric and AES symmetric encryption, with a stream message and component format using a TCP/IP stack for communications can be swapped for a provider that implements elliptic curve asymmetric and triple DES symmetric encryption, a bitmap message format and X.25 network communications, with a simple change of a configuration or command line option.

Code Generation

Spi2Java emits code for each Spi process definition in a method that is named after that definition. The Java code segments for all binding Spi processes, i.e. those that result in the substitution of a name value for a variable, are emitted inline. For example the Spi pair splitting process, $let\,(x, y) = M\,in\,P$, maps to the Java code segment (discussed in detail later):

```
// let (x, y) = M in
final <TypeX> x;
final <TypeY> y;
{
    InputStream _is =
      new ByteArrayInputStream(
        M.getData());
    x = getImpl().unpackNonce(
        _is);
    y = getImpl().unpackIdentifier(
        _is);
}
// Code for process P...
```

Making a method call, instead of emitting code inline, to implement this process would look something like

```
// let (x, y) = M in
<TypeX> x;
<TypeY> y;
split(&x, &y, M);
// Code for process P...
```

in C++. However this is not possible in Java as it does not have language support for "out parameters" (or pointers to pointers in C++ parlance) which would be required to assign values to the variables *x* and *y*. Using wrapper classes to encapsulate these variables, in lieu of out parameters, is a possible alternative, but would introduce an extra level of complexity to the code, as well as cluttering it with method calls instantiate wrappers and to set and get values from the wrapper instances.

Names of temporary variables required by some code segments are re-used in inlined code segments throughout the emitted code. Re-use is possible by declaring and operating on temporary variables in locally nested scopes. The nested scopes are introduced by a new Java block declared by the "*{*" and "*}*" symbols, as demonstrated in the pair splitting code segment listing. This approach is preferable to the alternatives: inlining code without nesting it in a new scope, requiring the use of arbitrarily large numbers of temporary variable names, which introduces extra logic to the code generator in order track them, or making method calls, which introduces new scope, but for the reasons discussed previously is not a viable alternative.

Using methods calls instead of inlined code segment would also break the safe practice of declaring all Java variables that correspond to Spi variables as *final*, meaning they can only be assigned to once, which faithfully implements the Spi model of processes substituting variables with name values as they run.

Spi Process to Java Mapping

Spi2Java uses the mappings defined in this subsection to generate Java code from Spi processes. As mentioned, the specification of these mappings is properly defined by the Prolog rules which associate each Spi process type with a Java code segment template. The Prolog direct clause grammar rules manage parsing the Spi processes, and each such rule has sub-rules that generate the Java code segment to be emitted from the associated code template.

Spi2Java also emits code to trace the protocol progress and state by means of updating a user interface. The interface also provides the user with a way control the run of protocol role, by stepping through the Spi processes that define it. In the Java code segment listings that follow we omit the tracing code for the purposes of clarity and brevity.

Output, $c!\langle N\rangle.P$, maps to a call to the *void spi.Protocol.send(spp.Channel, spp.Term)* method with the parameters channel c, the channel for communication, and term N, the term to be communicated. The code emitted for this process is thus:

```
// c!<N>.
send(c, N);
// Code for process P...
```

The parameters c and N may be Java variables, or expressions, that evaluate to values of types *spp.Channel* and *spp.Term* respectively.

Input, $c?(x).P$, maps to a call to the *Term spi.Protocol.recv(spp.Channel)* method, which is passed c as the channel parameter and returns a type that is of, or extends, *spp.Term*. The emitted code is of the form:

```
// c?(x).
final <Type> x =
   getImpl().unpack<Type>(recv(c)));
// Code for process P...
```

where *<Type>* is the type of the variable x and is determined by a lookup table that the code generator creates from the specification's variable type preamble.

Restriction, (n), is used to model nonce and timestamp creation and maps to a call to either *spp.Nonce spi.Protocol.newNonce( )* or *spp.Timestamp spi.Protocol.newTimestamp( )* depending on the type, again determined from the lookup table, of the variable n. Thus if n is of type *nonce* the code generator emits code of the form:

```
// (n)
Nonce n = newNonce();
// Code for process P...
```

or, if n is of type *time*, code of the form:

```
// (n)
Timestamp n = newTimestamp();
// Code for process P...
```

to implement this process.

Term Matching, $[M is N]P$, is mapped to a return statement that is guarded by checking a call to *boolean spi.Protocol.match(Term, Term)*:

```
// [m is n]
if (!match(m, n))
{
    return;
}
// Code for process P...
```

The method *boolean spi.Protocol.match(Term, Term)* is implemented as follows:

```
protected final boolean match(
    final Term a,
    final Term b)
{
    return a.match(b);
}
```

The method relies on the correctness of the provider's implementation of the *boolean spp.Term.match(Term)*method on the *spp.Term* interface. Implementations must return a boolean value indicating whether the parameter the method is called with, is equal to the instance it is called on.

Pair Splitting, *let* $(x, y) = M$ *in* P, is implemented by extracting the raw data from the Java *spp.Term* instance corresponding to the Spi term M. The two terms, x and y, that M is to be split into are then unpacked from this data.

To make it easier for the provider implementation to pack and unpack terms from raw data, we introduce a restriction on creating and splitting pairs that states that the first term must always be a name or name variable (i.e. it must be an atomic value). This restriction means that when the provider code packs and unpacks terms to send and receive over the communications network, it does not need to store extra information about the structure of the pairs - which may be nested to arbitrary depth, e.g. the message $\{A, B, C\}\, pub(A)$ would be specified $\{(A, (B, C))\}\, pub(A)$ given that A and B are names or name variables.

Apart from simplicity, this restriction has the advantage of making it possible to implement providers that are message compatible with existing security protocol implementations, as such implementations are unlikely to use pairing to structure their message data.

The Java code segment for this process is thus:

```
// let (x, y) = M in
final <TypeX> x;
final <TypeY> y;
{
    InputStream _is =
      new ByteArrayInputStream(
        M.getData());
    x = getImpl().unpackNonce(
        _is);
    y = getImpl().unpackIdentifier(
        _is);
}
// Code for process P...
```

where *<TypeX>* and *<TypeY>* are the types of the variables *x* and *y* respectively.

Decryption, *case L of* $\{x\}N$ *in P*, maps to a call to *InputStream spi.Protocol.decrypt(spp.Encryption, spp.Key)*. This call will propagate down to the *public byte[] spp.Key.decrypt(byte[])* method that is implemented by the provider according encryption algorithm associated with the type of key i.e. either symmetric, public or private.

```
// case L of {x}N in
final <Type> x =
    getImpl().unpack<Type>(
        decrypt(L, N));
// Code for process P...
```

5.   Implementation Example

To demonstrate Spi2Java we generate an implementation from the Spi specification of the Needham-Schroeder protocol, and the attack on it, given earlier. We list some sample generated code and then look at a run of a successful attacked on the protocol using the generated code for the initiator, responder and attacker roles.

The generated code for the *Init* process, which specifies the initiator role of the protocol, is given by the listing in Figure 4. Again, code generated for tracing and state monitoring, and some generated comments, have been omitted. Some minor formatting changes have also been made to facilitate typesetting.

Figure 5 shows a screenshot of the traces and final states of concurrent initiator, responder and attack runs of the Needham-Schroeder protocol roles. The implementation of each role's process prints the time of execution and the specification of each action to the trace window. Each process also updates the state window whenever a variable is substituted with a value.

The screenshots - showing the final states of the initiator, responder and attacker runs - clearly demonstrate that the attacker has subverted the protocol by gaining possession of the nonces m and n which the responder believes to be suitable shared secrets between himself and the initiator. Thus the attacker can masquerade as the initiator. Should the responder base the confidentiality and/or authenticity of continued communication with the party he believes to be initiator, the attacker will be able to continue this charade.

6.   Current Work

While we have addressed the issue of verifying Spi2Java in terms of correctly performing the specified mappings from Spi to Java code, the issue of the correctness of those mappings needs to be resolved. We are currently working on showing that the mappings preserve the Spi semantics in the Java code and will correct any mapping definitions that fail to do so.

Our approach will follow the refinement methodology and involve setting up, and satisfying, proof obligations for each Java code segment. This entails relating Spi semantics to those of the Java language. While there is no official formal semantics for the Java language, an Abstract State Machine (also referred to as evolving algebras) semantics has been defined in [BS99]. We intend to use this definition of Java for this process along with the transition semantics defined for the Spi Calculus.

Successfully completing this task will allow us to meet the second requirement for high integrity code generation identified in [WH99] which states *"The translation between a specification expressed in a source language and a*

```
// Init(c, A, B) =
public void Init(final Channel c, final Identifier A,
    final Identifier B)
{
    final Nonce n = newNonce(); // (n)
    // c!<{(n, A)}pub(B)>.
    send(c, encrypt(newPair(n, A), pub(B)));
    // c?(1).
    final Encryption l = getImpl().unpackEncryption(
        recv(c));
    // case l of {j}priv(A) in
    final Term j = getImpl().unpackTerm(
        decrypt(l, priv(A)));
    // let (x, m) = j in
    final Nonce x; final Nonce m;
    {
        InputStream _is = new ByteArrayInputStream(
            j.getData());
        x = getImpl().unpackNonce(_is);
        m = getImpl().unpackNonce(_is);
    }
    // [x is n]
    if (!match(x, n)) return;
    // c!<{m}pub(B)>.
    send(c, encrypt(m, pub(B)));
    // nil
    return;
}
```

Figure 4.   Generated code for the Needham-Schroeder initiator role.

program expressed in a target language must be formal and proven to maintain
the meaning of the specification."

7.   Conclusion

In this paper we have described our approach to bridging the gap between
security protocol specification and implementation using the Spi2Java code
generation tool. We have shown that by a using formal specification language,
the Spi Calculus, and implementing Spi2Java in a logic programming language, Prolog, we can progress towards the ultimate goal of meeting Whalen
and Heimdahl's requirements for high integrity code generation. Further to

Figure 5. Concurrent runs of Spi2Java generated implementations of the Needham-Schroeder participant roles and attack.

this goal, the approach to our current work - validating the refinement of the Spi Calculus processes to Java code - is briefly outlined. Despite this validation not being complete, we list the mappings from Spi processes to Java code segments that Spi2Java currently uses. This acts not only as a reference for the potential user but also to highlight the relative simplicity of the mappings.

The separation of protocol logic implementation from cryptographic and network specific implementation concerns by the SPP API, contributes to implementation correctness, by allowing Spi2Java to be focused on just the protocol logic aspect and not on lower level abstractions which would make the generated code far more complex.

Finally we demonstrate the potential of Spi2Java by using it to implement not only the legitimate roles of the Needham-Schroeder protocol, but also the attacker role described by Lowe. These implementations are executed concurrently to give a trace of a successful run of the attack on the protocol.

We believe that the above indicates that using a more formal and automated approach to implementing network security protocols simplifies the process and reduces the potential for errors. Hence it adds value to the process of security protocol development as a whole.

References

[AG98]   M. Abadi and A.D. Gordon. A Calculus for Cryptographic Protocols: The Spi Calculus. Technical Report SRC Research Report 149, Digital Systems Research Centre, 1998.

[BS99]   E. Borger and W. Schulte. A programmer friendly modular definition of the semantics of java. In J. Alves-Foss, editor, *Formal Syntax and Semantics of Java, volume 1523 of Lect. Notes in Comp. Sci.*, pages 353–404. Springer-Verlag, 1999.

[CERa]   CERT. CERTő Advisory CA-2003-26 Multiple Vulnerabilities in SSL/TLS Implementations.

[CERb]   CERT. Microsoft private communication technology (pct) fails to properly validate message inputs.

[CERc]   CERT. Vulnerability Note VU#104280 Multiple vulnerabilities in SSL/TLS implementations.

[CHP90]   J. Bowen C.A.R. Hoare, H. Jifeng and P. Pandya. ESPRIT BRA 3104 ProCoS project: Provably Correct Systems. Technical report, Oxford University Computing Laboratory, 1990.

[Cra03]   F. Crazzolara. *Language, Semantics, and Methods for Security Protocols.* PhD thesis, University of Aarhus, 2003.

[Den00]   G. Denker. Design of a CIL connector to Maude. In N. Heintze H. Veith and E. Clarke, editors, *Workshop on Formal Methods and Comuter Security.* Carnegie Mellon University, July 2000.

[Did]   X. Didelot. COSP-J: A Compile for Security Protocols. Master's thesis, University of Oxford.

[DPD04]   Riccardo Sisto Davide Pozza and Luca Durante. Spi2Java: Automatic Cryptographic ProtocolJava Code Generation from spi calculus. In *18th International Conference on Advanced Information Networking and Applications (AINA'04) Volume 1*, page 400. IEEE, 2004.

[DXSP01]   Adrian Perrig Dawn Xiaodong Song and Doantam Phan. AGVI - Automatic Generation, Verification, and Implementation of Security Protocols. In *Proceedings of the 13th International Conference on Computer Aided Verification*, pages 241–245. Springer-Verlag, 2001.

[DY81]   D. Dolev and A.C. Yao. On the security of public key protocols. Technical report, Stanford University, 1981.

[KDE]   KDE. KDE Security Advisory: KDE 2.2 / Konqueror Embedded SSL vulnerability.

[LGY90]   R. Needham L. Gong and R. Yahalom. Reasoning about belief in cryptographic protocols. In Deborah Cooper and Teresa Lunt, editors, *Proceedings 1990 IEEE Symposium on Research in Security and Privacy*, pages 234–248. IEEE Computer Society, 1990.

[Low95]   G. Lowe. An attack on the needham-schroeder public-key authentication protocol. *Information Processing Letters*, 56(3):131–133, 1995.

[Low96]   G. Lowe. Breaking and fixing the Needham-Schroeder public-key protocol using FDR. In *Tools and Algorithms for the Construction and Analysis of Systems (TACAS)*, volume 1055, pages 147–166. Springer-Verlag, Berlin Germany, 1996.

[MBN96]   M. Abadi M. Burrows and R. Needham. A logic of authentication, from proceedings of the royal society, volume 426, number 1871, 1989. In *William Stallings, Practical Cryptography for Data Internetworks*. IEEE Computer Society Press, 1996.

[MM01]   J. Millen and F. Muller. Cryptographic protocol generation from CAPSL. Technical Report SRI-CSL-01-07, SRI International, December 2001.

[Mor98]   C. Morgan. *Programming from specifications (2nd ed.)*. Prentice Hall International (UK) Ltd., 1998.

[MPW92]   Robin Milner, Joachim Parrow, and David Walker. A calculus of mobile processes, Parts I and II. *Journal of Information and Computation*, 100(1):1–40 and 41–77, 1992.

[PYS03]   C. R. Ramakrishnan Ping Yang and Scott A. Smolka. A logical encoding of the pi-calculus: Model checking mobile processes using tabled resolution. In *Verification, Model Checking and Abstract Interpretation (VMCAI)*, volume 2575 of *Lecture Notes in Computer Science*, pages 116–131, New York, NY, January 2003. Springer.

[SGS95]   SGS-THOMSON Microelectronics Limited. *Occam 2.1 reference manual*, 1995.

[THG99]   J. Thayer, J. Herzog, and J. Guttman. Strand spaces: Proving security protocols correct. *Journal of Computer Security*, 1999.

[WH99]   M.W. Whalen and M.P.E. Heimdahl. On the requirements of high-integrity code generation. In *Proceedings of the Fourth IEEE High Assurance in Systems Engineering Workshop*, November 1999.

[Wie03]   J. Wielemaker. SWI-Prolog 5.2.10 Reference Manual, 2003.

USING NGSCB TO MITIGATE EXISTING SOFTWARE THREATS

Matt Barrett

mbar116@ec.auckland.ac.nz
Department of Computer Science
The University of Auckland

Clark Thomborson

cthombor@cs.auckland.ac.nz
Department of Computer Science
The University of Auckland

Abstract   We introduce Microsoft's Next-Generation Secure Computing Base (*NGSCB*), and present a novel metaphor to describe it. An existing software application providing electronic legal document services is discussed, and results of a security analysis presented. The existing software architecture is extended with NGSCB to solve some noted security vulnerabilities. The novel architecture is then analysed for its successes and shortcomings.

1.   Introduction

Microsoft is being watched with considerable interest as they continue to promote and develop their Next-Generation Secure Computing Base, alongside other industry heavyweights developing trusted computing platforms [TCG03a]. Commentators are weighing in, with both technical [Spi03] and philosophical [Sta02] arguments against the innovations being promoted by the Trusted Computing Group.

Whilst the debate surrounding the various philosophical and technical implications of NGSCB, and trusted computing as a whole, is being fiercely conducted, little has been said or done about its possible uses when integrated with existing applications.

It is expected by the authors that NGSCB will first appear in commercial desktops. This prediction is made based on the observation that the benefits of NGSCB will appeal most strongly to businesses that have an interest in conducting more secure electronic transactions with other businesses.

Conversely, it is also expected by the authors that NGSCB will find resistance in the home market. The same features that allow a company to secure its data and operations from an attack can be used to remove existing privileges that home users have with digital content. A home environment with an NGSCB-enabled system would enable content providers to implement powerful DRM systems, allowing secure end-to-end digital media delivery to the home [Bre01].

Previous attempts at securing digital content in a hostile environment have failed, and researchers attempting to secure software from modification or unauthorised duplication have stated that a successful solution without a hardware component is not possible [MP01]. Microsoft will make use of the Trusted Platform Module (TPM) [TCG03a] designed by the Trusted Computing Group, manufactured and provided by hardware vendors, including AMD [Str03], to fill the role of this hardware component.

This paper presents a case study investigating the application of NGSCB to an existing software application. For NGSCB to prove useful to software developers with an existing product, it should be able to be integrated into an existing architecture without requiring extensive modifications. Indeed, if the modifications required to integrate NGSCB necessitate significant changes to the code base, it may be more cost effective for a development team to design and implement their own security enhancements, as opposed to using the more general, yet perhaps stronger, toolset provided by NGSCB.

The application chosen for this case study was Electronic Legal Forms (ELF) [ELF03], a product of the Auckland District Law Society (ADLS) [ADL03]. The Electronic Legal Forms application allows lawyers to work with electronic versions of pre-prepared legal documents. The Auckland District Law Society's hard-copy legal form product provide law firms in New Zealand with standardised, well-known documents to assist them in various legal transactions. It should be noted that the architecture described in this case study requires all involved parties to have NGSCB-enabled platforms.

This paper is organised as follows. The second section will introduce NGSCB, illustrating some features and describing its operation through use of a novel metaphor. The third section will describe the Electronic Legal Forms software. Its purpose, features and security vulnerabilities and the security goals of integration with NGSCB will be outlined. The fourth section presents an integrated architecture, and illustrates possible uses of NGSCB. Section five contains discussion of the success and shortcomings of the NGSCB integration.

2. Microsoft's NGSCB

A detailed analysis of the Next-Generation Secure Computing Base is outside the scope of this paper. A good introduction to NGSCB can be found on Microsoft's NGSCB webpage [Mic03b].

Novel Security Primitives

NGSCB provides four new security primitives to Windows application developers, through a number of hardware modifications described in [Mic03a] by Microsoft. These four new security primitives are sealed storage, secure IO, strong process isolation and attestation.

Attestation is the most novel of these four security primitives. It allows the security boundary from a nexus computing agent (NCA) running on one machine to extend to and include that of another NCA running on another machine, with communication taking place over an insecure channel such as the Internet. Further explanation of attestation, and nexus computing agents, can be found in section 2. In brief, this allows applications to trust a remote application to perform in a correct manner, despite it being located on a machine administered by possibly malicious users. Using this base, policy projection from one computer to another can occur, enabling Digital Rights Management (DRM) style applications to be built.

It is described as the most novel, because of all four new security primitives provided by NGSCB, it alone enables a new class of secure application to be built. Sealed storage simply advances upon features that come from file systems with access control, but shifts authorisation from being derived from the identity of the user to being derived from the identity of the program. Secure input and output are novel features, but do not allow new applications to be built until secure peripherals, other than video, mouse, and keyboard become available. Additionally, there are already a number of software-only methods available to prevent screen scraping in Microsoft Windows. Strong process isolation merely provides in hardware what has been provided in some degree by operating systems for a number of years. Whilst it makes virtual memory protection much more secure, most current applications are written on the assumption that their memory address range is protected from other programs.

Attestation, however, allows remote cryptographic verification of not only the executing program but also the call stack, all the way down to the hardware level. This is a powerful new security primitive, creating new levels of assurance for computations performed by remote computers, and allowing administrators to project policy to remote platforms. Attestation is described in various levels of detail by England et al and in the various white papers [TCG03b, ELMW03, Mic03d] published by Microsoft [Mic03b]. It makes use of a Trusted Platform Module (TPM), along with various cryptographic certificates, to prove that a specific hardware and software stack is NGSCB-enabled, and can be trusted to operate as expected.

A Hierarchy of Trust

Figure 1.   A Three-Layer Hierachy

Without a strong technical understanding of NGSCB, it can be difficult to imagine how the system will operate when in widespread use. As is often the case with technical subjects, it is useful to develop a metaphor for the NGSCB system. The NGSCB environment that runs inside a single machine can be thought of as a hierarchy of three enforcement agents. The enforcement agents running inside a system have differing levels of authority. They are identified by their badge numbers, which are generated for each agent, by the agent directly above it in the hierarchy.

The badge number can be thought of as a code ID or manifest. This is a hash of the binary executable of the program. The TPM hardware chip can be thought of as a police officer; an executing nexus can be thought of as a security guard; an executing NCA can be thought of as an ordinary citizen. This three-layer hierarchy is illustrated in Figure 1.

The nexus is the trusted kernel that hosts those programs specifically written to take advantage of NGSCB security primitives. These are referred to as nexus computing agents (NCAs), and run separately from both other NCAs and normal programs.

The police officer can be trusted to enforce the operating restrictions of NGSCB as it is fixed in hardware. The police officer's validity is proven by the certificate of the manufacturer, which it can provide upon request. This certificate attests that it has been built to an approved, published standard.

The police officer, or TPM, will allow any security guard, or nexus, to run on the platform. The police officer can be guaranteed to provide, when asked, the correct badge number of the security guard, which can be used to ensure that the security guard is who he claims to be. In turn, the security guard will attest to the identity of any citizen, or NCA, it is watching or hosting.

When using the seal primitive, the three identities of the police officer, security guard, and citizen work together. In the common case, of a citizen sealing secrets to itself for later use, their unique identities ensure that the data can only be unsealed when the same police officer, security guard, and citizen are present. This means the data cannot be unsealed on a different NGSCB platform, where the police officer, or TPM, differs. It also means that the security guard and citizen will be the same executing binaries when the data was sealed, as when it is unsealed.

Despite the open nature of the NGSCB system, that according to Microsoft will allow anyone to write a nexus and NCA themselves [Gra03], this hierarchy of identities will remove some of the freedom of choice that may initially appear to be present. Users must run security guards whose identities are known by the parties to whom they are attesting. This can be easily illustrated by describing a current application that could make use of attestation — securing online banking — described in [Mic03d].

The bank server, running under a known police officer and a known security guard, receives the attestation vector from the remote client bank application. The vector contains the identity of the application, or citizen, as well as the identity of the security guard under which it is running. These identities are certified by the signature of the police officer, who is implemented in hardware and is considered trusted by all parties. An alternative is that the two identities are certified by a third party, who is trusted by the bank to only issue certifications to NGSCB platforms — this process allows some degree of anonymity. The bank server will only communicate with the remote application if both the identities of the security guard and the application are as expected.

In effect, NGSCB places a police officer inside the current PC architecture that can be trusted to ensure that the operation of any security guard or citizen is assured, and cannot be modified during execution. The end user is in full control over what security guards and citizens are allowed to run on their system, and what information the various entities can reveal. However, in order to make use of citizens, or NCAs, to obtain a service or perform some communication, a specific security guard, or nexus, must be running under the police officer. No details are available as to how many nexus will be made available for use. It is expected that a Microsoft-written nexus will be distributed, and used by default. It will be this security guard that citizens (provided by software vendors) will need to run under, in order to be identified correctly.

3.   Electronic Legal Forms

Business Usage

The Auckland District Law Society's Electronic Legal Forms application is intended for use by lawyers and legal professionals to prepare legal forms for use in a variety of transactions. The product was developed seven years ago to allow law offices to move away from the dated practice of legal secretaries working with manual typewriters, filling in the various fields of a hard-copy legal form template. The user is able to work with an electronic version of the template, filling in the required fields and removing clauses that are not required for a specific document. By moving to an electronic format, forms can be partially completed, returned to later, and then finalised before printing and signing by the client.

ELF Features

In the current implementation, electronic stock is stored on a hardware dongle attached to the user's computer, or in the case of larger firms on a network server. This dongle is referred to as a Software Authentication Button (SAB). The Electronic Legal Forms application connects to the SAB whenever a final copy of the document is printed. The software ensures that sufficient reserves of stock are present on the SAB. The stock is decremented by the appropriate amount, and the legal form is printed. This process allows collection of revenue by the ADLS.

The Electronic Legal Forms package allows users of the software to send under-revision, or finalised, copies of documents to each other. The editing process is conducted through a GUI, shown in Figure 2. User-modifiable fields are shown in grey, and boilerplate legalese is viewable as black-on-white text.

After creating or editing a legal form, users simply transmit a string, obtained from ELF, which encodes only the fields that contain user-modifiable text, through e-mail to the other party. There, the encoded string is inserted into Electronic Legal Forms. For example, the name and address of one party can be entered by their lawyer, after which the document can be sent to the lawyer of another party, who can update the required fields with their own client's name and address. Once the legal form has been finalised to all parties' satisfaction, the form is marked as such. After this point in time, ELF no

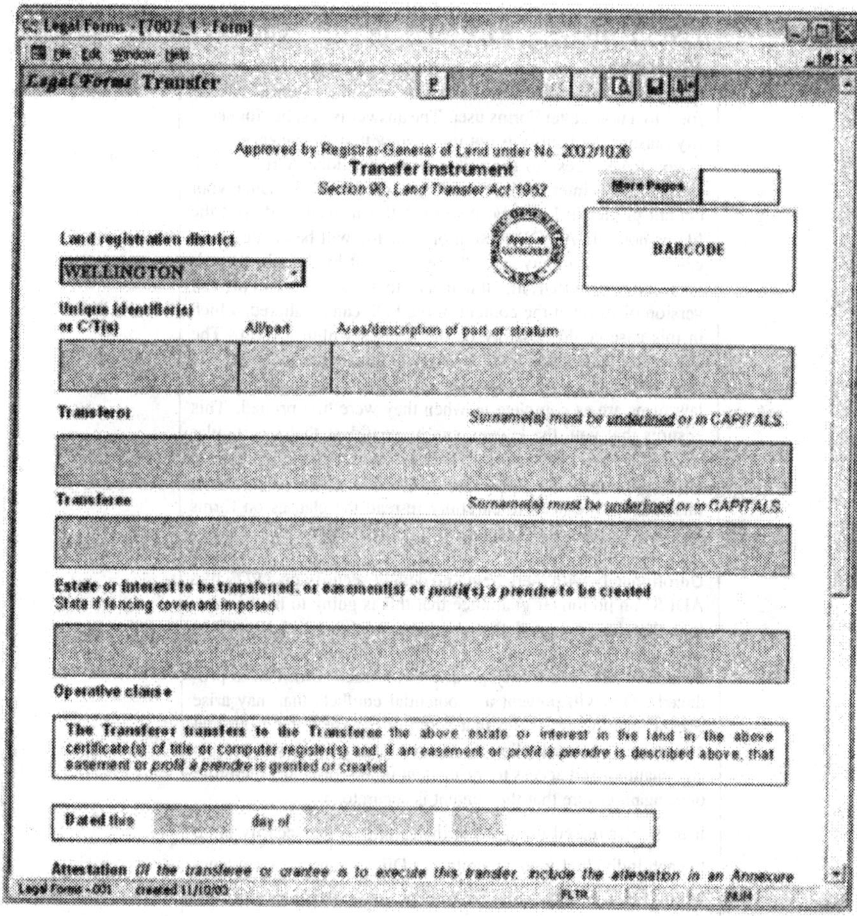

Figure 2. Electronic Legal Forms interface

longer allows modification to the user-modifiable fields. This process requires a copy of Electronic Legal Forms at both ends of the communication, as the information that makes up the body of the legal form — information that should be a facsimile across all versions of that legal form — is not transmitted.

Security Goals

The implementation described above illustrates an important design goal of Electronic Legal Forms. The exact wording and formatting of a legal document is of the utmost importance.

EMAILING   ELECTRONIC   LEGAL FORMS

Many users have asked whether it is possible to email a legal form to a non Legal Forms user. The answer is yes, but for security reasons the facility is not included within the package.

If you have access to the full version of Adobe Acrobat, or a simple PDF printer driver, then all you need to do is change your default printer in Legal Forms to use this instead, and print the file as normal. A PDF version of your file will be created, and can be emailed to anyone. Please note that by default, there is no security on a PDF file, this means that with access to the full version of Acrobat the content of the PDF can be altered, which in this case could possibly be the clauses within a form. The amended file can then be re-saved with the alterations intact.

For ADLS it is paramount that any forms distributed between law firms are as complete as when they were first printed. This ensures that you, the lawyer, can be confident that a particular word of a particular clause will always appear in the same place on the same page each and every time. Being able to guarantee this reduces the need to carefully re-read the clauses on forms that may be printed or received from other lawyers, unless absolutely necessary.

Unfortunately with there being no default security on a PDF file, ADLS can no longer guarantee that this is going to be the case. It is therefore essential that if anyone wishes to create a PDF version of the form using one of these methods, that they independently set the security passwords on each form that is produced. This will prevent any potential conflicts that may arise over a form being signed that could otherwise differ from that originally generated. Setting the security options will prevent any unauthorised access to the content of the form, and therefore once again ensure that the content is accurate.

It must be stressed though that the setting of the security is up to each individual who generates a PDF version of a form from within Legal Forms, and ADLS are not responsible for the content of the form once it leaves the package in PDF format.

Figure 3. Instructions to ELF users taken from August 2003 Auckland District Law Society newsletter

Legal forms that include the Auckland District Law Society letterhead are widely accepted amongst lawyers as being correct replications, and are favoured because they do not require proof reading at each use. The Auckland District Law Society guarantees the veracity of their legal forms supplied in hard copy format, and of final copies that are printed directly from the Electronic Legal Forms package.

This is one of the primary goals of the ADLS, and can be found in their own words in paragraph 4 of Figure 3. From this, a security goal that users of ELF, after NGSCB integration, are able to transmit documents in a format whose veracity can be guaranteed by the ADLS is derived. This is defined as

$G1$ in table Table 1. This is a goal of the (non-malicious) lawyers who use ELF (hereafter referred to as primary users). It is also a goal of the (non-malicious) secondary users, defined as those with whom a primary user communicates but does not have an ELF installation. It is not strictly a goal of the ADLS, but due to interest in their clients' satisfaction, may be considered one.

The ADLS also requires the payment of an appropriate fee for each legal form that is printed. Again, the implementation described in section 3 allows the ADLS to collect the appropriate fees for each printed hard copy of a legal form. This is defined as $G2$ in Table 1. This goal is only pertinent to the ADLS, as primary or secondary users of ELF are not strictly concerned that revenue is collected for each print.

The Auckland District Law Society recently noted an increase in requests from clients to be able to email copies of legal forms to users who do not have ELF. This issue was addressed in an August 2003 newsletter, the relevant parts of which are reproduced in Figure 3. The ADLS is concerned that PDF is seen by many as a way to send a high quality document that cannot be easily modified to others. These requests lead the ADLS to look for a document format that can be transmitted like a PDF, yet retain goals $G1$ and $G2$. This goal is defined as $G3$, in Table 1. This is a goal of both primary and secondary users of ELF as it allows them to communicate. Again, this is not strictly a goal of the ADLS, but for the same reasons as $G1$, may be considered one.

Currently, printing to PDF from Electronic Legal Forms is possible using standard PDF printer drivers. Paragraph 2 of Figure 3 instructs ELF users how they may print to the PDF format. Paragraph 3 points out to users that there is no default security in a PDF file. Despite user education, the Auckland District Law Society is concerned that its users may enjoy a false sense of security regarding the static nature of a document printed to PDF. Without the appropriate security restrictions put in place at the time of authoring, a PDF can be modified with ease. The Auckland District Law Society is aware of this, and is not willing to provide the same guarantees to a document's veracity once it has been transmitted in PDF format over an open channel. Paragraphs 4 and 5 of Figure 3 show that the ADLS strongly deprecate the use of PDF to transmit legal forms.

An additional security concern, inherent in electronic communication, is the ease with which a confidential legal document can be sent via e-mail to unauthorised parties. Working with only hard copies of legal documents severely restricts the distribution of highly confidential information to unauthorised parties, both by accident and through malice. If the use of PDF to store and transport legal documents via email increases, mistaken or malicious transmission to unauthorised third parties will also increase. It is viewed as highly beneficial by the ADLS [MM03] to be able to impart DRM-style viewing restrictions to an authored document. Ideally, a closed set of relevant parties could be added to a legal document, with other parties unable to view the document. This is defined as $G4$ in Table 1. This is a goal of both the primary and secondary users of ELF. Again, it is not strictly a goal of the ADLS, but due to interest in their clients' satisfaction, may be considered one.

It is worth drawing comparisons between the security goals outlined in Table 1, obtained by analysis of ELF, and Pfleeger's [Pfl97] three arms of computer security: confidentiality, integrity, and availability (CIA). Goal $G1$ maps directly to the integrity of the legal form. Goal $G2$ is a special case of Pfleeger's availability — a restricted DRM-style availability. Goal $G3$ is a standard availability goal. Goal $G4$ is a confidentiality goal. This CIA mnemonic will be used in section 5 to draw conclusions about the success or failure of the proposed architecture to satisfy the stated security goals.

Security Threats

In the current ELF architecture, certain threats to the defined security goals arise due to an ability to print to the PDF format from within Electronic Legal Forms. Additionally, a number of threats arise from the manner in which a legal form is transmitted between two users of ELF, as described in 3.2 above.

It is possible to prevent the installation of printer drivers on an administered Windows machine, and thus restrict the ability to print to PDF from Electronic Legal Forms through a PDF printer driver. However, this form of restriction is not possible when the program is installed on machines not under the administration of the Auckland District Law Society.

A PDF document can be re-printed without any limitations by anyone who obtains it. As described previously, the transferral to hard copy of an electronic legal form is a considerable and important source of revenue for the Auckland District Law Society. The ease of printing to PDF from Electronic Legal Forms allows two paths for violation of $G2$ (Table 1).

The first is the casual printing of a legal form that has been sent to a secondary user by a primary user, or a malicious third party who happens upon the document through other channels. They are able to print a copy for themselves, indistinguishable from a copy printed directly from Electronic Legal Forms for which revenue was collected. The print operation occurs outside the control of an ELF installation, resulting in an inability to collect revenue for the print. This is noted as $T1$ in Table 1. A print operation is considered controlled if the appropriate fee is paid at some point.

The second comes from the removal of the personalised text, such as names and addresses, from the PDF. This process, performed only once, creates a blank template. This template can be used to avoid the need to purchase legal forms from the Auckland District Law Society. This threat is noted as $T2$ in

Table 1. This threat comes from primary and secondary users, as well as from malicious third parties.

In addition to allowing printing without restriction, a standard PDF file also allows modification of the document itself. This opens the document up to threats $T3$ (modification of the legalese boilerplate, as defined in section 3), and $T4$ (modification of the user-modifiable fields). These threats come from a malicious third party who is able to intercept, modify and re-inject the document on its way from a primary to a secondary user through an insecure channel. Additionally, primary and secondary users are able to modify the document, calling into question the accuracy of both parties' copies.

In comparison, transmission between two or more users of ELF (section 3), where the legal form is never printed to PDF, results in only $T4$ able to occur. In this situation, only primary users are involved in the transmission of the legal form. In fact, it should be noted that if a form is never printed to PDF threats $T1$ and $T2$ can not occur. However, as previously mentioned, it is impossible to prevent a legal form from being printed to PDF. This issue is addressed in section 5. It is possible, however, for the string transmitted between two primary users across an insecure channel to be modified by a malicious third party able to intercept, modify and reinject it. This is noted as $T4$ in Table 1.

4. Integrated Design

To make full use of the security that can be implemented with NGSCB, a Public Key Infrastructure (PKI) built around NGSCB is proposed. Then an NGSCB-enabled legal form viewer that allows controlled distribution of legal forms is described. Finally, a simple architecture for allowing controlled remote printing to occur is described.

PKI and Attestation

Many of the weaknesses of a PKI come from being unable to control the enrolment of parties into the scheme, and being unable to verify their identities when doing so. With Electronic Legal Forms, administered enrolment is possible when a copy of the software is purchased and installed by a law firm. When discussing the new design of the ELF architecture it will be referred to as New ELF (NELF).

The root of trust is a master server Lf, or certificate authority, administered by the Auckland District Law Society. The installation procedure of a copy of NELF at a primary user's site involves the generation of a public/private key pair, k_i/k_i'. This key pair is for the sole intended use of participating in the ADLS controlled PKI. The private key is stored, using the NGSCB seal primitive [Mic03d], on the local computer, C_{local}.

GOALS

	Description	Goal Of
G1	"...a particular word of a particular clause will always appear in the same place on the same page..."	Non-malicious primary and secondary users
G2	Every print operation of a legal form is controlled by the ADLS, allowing collection of the appropriate revenue	ADLS
G3	A legal form can be viewed on a computer without an ELF installation.	Primary user, secondary user
G4	A legal form can only be read by the intended recipient(s)	Non-malicious primary and secondary users

THREATS

	Description	Threat From
T1	Uncontrolled printing of a finalised form	Primary and secondary users, and third parties
T2	Creation of an electronic template of a legal form	Primary and secondary users, and third parties
T3	Modification of the legalese boilerplate on a legal form.	Malicious third parties, and malicious primary and secondary parties
T4	Modification of the user-modifiable fields on a legal form	Malicious third parties, and malicious primary and secondary parties.

Table 1. Security goals and threats of ELF

Once this is done, the newly installed copy of NELF contacts the ADLS server. The procedure for establishing a trust relationship between two NCAs on different computers is described in the Microsoft white paper concerning software authentication [Mic03c]. In this situation, the two NCAs in question are the ADLS administered NGSCB-enabled NELF server, and newly installed NELF NCA on the primary user's computer.

One difficulty with automatically creating a trust relationship between a NELF installation and the ADLS server is establishing network communication in heterogeneous corporate environments. A secure communication is required between the two parties who are expected to be located behind various layers of network and application security. It is feasible to perform the required communication over the HTTPS protocol — which is widely available on corporate desktops, and allowed through corporate firewalls.

An initial communication takes place, most likely over HTTPS. The HTTPS protocol ensures the integrity of the communication, and the confidentiality. The primary user, through checking the server's PKI certificate, will authenticate the server. For this communication, the previously generated public key, k_i, is attested by the nexus running on the primary user's computer. It is then transmitted, along with other cryptographic information used to verify the NGSCB platform itself and the NELF installation program to the ADLS server. This extra information is used to verify that the NCAs that are communicating with each other can be trusted to operate as expected, i.e. they are executing on a valid NGSCB platform, as described previously in section 2 above.

The ADLS server signs a certificate, C_k, identifying the public key, along with information concerning the primary user itself, A_i, most likely a contact address or other information of interest to users. This certificate is returned to the NCA at the primary user's site. In order for identification to be established in both directions, the process is repeated, with the two NCAs reversing their roles. Once this process has been completed for the primary user, it is considered enrolled into the ADLS PKI. This protocol is outlined more succinctly in Table 2, as PKI Enrolment and Attestation.

The NELF application is modified to present the identities of other primary users, A_x, who are enrolled into the PKI, when preparing a legal form for electronic transmission. This directory listing would be retrieved from the ADLS server when the primary user's NELF installation first enrols into the PKI, and periodically thereafter, to maintain a fresh listing. A legal form would then be encrypted with the published public key(s), k_x, of the respective primary user(s), A_x, to which it addressed.

Due to the forced enrolment during installation, and the inclusion of suitable identification information, future communications are able to take place between law firms in confidence. Revocation is controlled by the ADLS. Regular updates by primary users of their local certificate stores will reduce the likelihood of a compromised key continuing to be trusted.

Widget

Further integration of NGSCB with NELF occurs through the development of a widget, similar in functionality and use to Adobe's Acrobat Reader. This widget re-uses the internal document format and existing form editor of Electronic Legal Forms as shown in Figure 2.

As described previously, the current version of Electronic Legal Forms allows two users of the product to transfer under-revision or finalised legal forms between themselves. This functionality would not be removed when integrated with NGSCB, but would be restricted in order to address $G4$ — preventing viewing of a legal form by unauthorised parties — with a PKI as described in section 4.

PKI Enrolment and Attestation

1. Root of trust created on ADLS administered server Lf. Public/private key paid j/j' generated.
2. Installation of NELF at law firm. Public/private key pair k/k' generated, and stored on C_{local} with NGSCB *seal* command.
3. New NELF install contacts ADLS server over HTTPS. C_{local} nexus attests to k, Lf nexus attests to j.
4. Lf signs certificate C_{kn}, including A_{kn} and k. A_k contains enough information to uniquely identify the law firm, most likely with name and addresses.
5. C_{kn} returned to C_{local} along with all other C_k certificates created for other law firms.

Message Transmission

1. User picks certificate C_k of intended recipient from list presented, using A_k to identify them.
2. Legal form is encrypted with public key C_k, and emailed to electronic address specified in A_k.

Table 2. Protocol Steps

Lightweight DRM Wrapper

Currently, when a user wishes to send a legal form by email to a client they print the form to PDF, which is then emailed to the client. Under the new architecture, this process is still the same. However, instead of a PDF being generated, an encrypted version of the legal form is generated. This legal form can only be viewed with the NELF widget.

This NCA widget has a limited set of functions, and can enforce a number of restrictions, such as an inability to print the form. It is similar in appearance and usability to the document viewing and editing component of Electronic Legal Forms.

In order to ensure the confidentiality of the transmitted document ($G3$) additional trust relationships must be established. A trust relationship is established between a primary user (a law firm), Lf, that uses NELF and any secondary users (clients), Cl_{1-n}, to whom a legal document needed to be distributed. This would take a similarn form as between the PKI rooted at the ADLS administration server, and primary users using ELF.

The widget installation file from the primary user's NELF computer is distributed to the client. The client, $C1$, upon reception through email of the widget from a trusted party — namely their law firm Lf, simply executes it. It is expected that local user interaction and authorization will be required to allow an NCA to execute on a computer. The exact manner in which this will occur has not yet been finalised by Microsoft. Additionally, NCAs are likely

[CK03] to execute in a sandboxed environment, with a user-customisable set of restrictions placed upon them.

Once the user authorises the execution of the widget, a trust relationship must be formed between the secondary and primary users. The secondary user's NELF widget installation generates a public/private key pair, k/k'. The public key k of this pair is presented in an emailtransmittable form to the user. It is then emailed to the primary user Lf, which records the public key in their local ELF system. This process could easily be automated, so to appear transparent to the primary and secondary users. No trust relationship is established in the reverse direction, as none is required. The NELF viewer widget serves only to display the documents; it does not allow any editing or formatting to take place.

At this point, the widget has been installed, and the newly generated public key returned to Lf. The main NELF installation at Lf can then send legal forms encrypted with the appropriate public key of the intended recipient.

Documents are prepared for sending to secondary users with the installed widget, just as a form is currently prepared for printing to PDF. A primary user can create a copy of the legal document encrypted for the relevant secondary user. The NELF program would present a list of known widgets that have been distributed and installed. A primary user can select the secondary users to whom they want to distribute the document. The document would be encrypted, and the primary user would simply email the file to the secondary user. There, the preinstalled NCA widget would be used to display the document securely.

This procedure illustrates the ability to create a secure, one-way trust relationship between two NGSCB platforms without the need for a hierarchical PKI that is created by attestation. Once again, however, the NGSCB platform verifies the NCA has not been modified, and can be trusted to maintain the policies applied to any legal documents sent to it.

The architecture described here presumes all parties involved have NGSCB platforms upon which to execute the NCAs. This is a major shortcoming, and is noted in section 5.

This architecture illustrates the use of NGSCB to project policy restrictions onto a remote computer to protect an electronic document. It can be seen as a lightweight DRM application, capable of protecting high value documents, the integrity of which both parties have an interest in.

Printing and Replay Attacks

The design is further extended to allow $G2$ (the collection of revenue for all printed legal forms) to occur at secondary users' sites, as well as primary users'.

The secondary user is able to print a restricted number of copies of the legal form under certain conditions. When a document is being prepared for transmission to a secondary user, a certain number of print credits must be attached to the document by the primary user, if the secondary user is to print that document. The ADLS collects revenue for these credited prints from the NELF primary user's account. The primary user can collect the cost of these prints from their secondary user through their regular accounting channels with that user. When the document is viewed by the widget, the print credits allow the secondary user a set number of prints. When a copy is printed, the credits are decremented, and the document securely updated with the new value.

This method of enabling remote pay-per-print is vulnerable to a form of replay attack. A secondary user who receives a document that contains a certain number of print credits may simply exhaust those credits, then replace the exhausted copy with the document they were originally sent.

A solution to this attack is to force the widget to contact a server, run by the primary user that distributed the document, in order to verify every print command. There are a number of problems with this solution.

Firstly, a primary user may not want, or have the capability, to maintain a permanent presence on the Internet. Secondly, even if each primary user provided such a server, each print operation would require a network connection to the server, which may not be possible for a number of reasons. An ideal solution would have some form of offline printing capability, as well as still ensuring that $G2$ is maintained.

In the system described, the NCA widget is able to store some uniquely identifying attribute of any document for which it generates a printed copy in its configuration set. Future attempts to print the same file will be caught by matching the unique attribute previously stored. It can be seen that this merely shifts the target of any attempted replay attack. Now, the configuration set, which has data concerning the number of times a certain document has been printed, is simply replaced with an earlier copy.

Discussions with members of the NGSCB development team [RC03] regarding this problem revealed a number of solutions under development. One interesting idea was the development of an encrypted NGSCB registry, which NCAs could use to store persistent state. If this was modified or deleted, the NGSCB platform itself could be engineered to stop working, preventing further access to the legal documents. In addition, counters such as those required by the NELF widget could be stored in multiple places, increasing the difficulty of simply replacing them with earlier values. While these solutions would not make the described replay attack impossible, it would increase the difficulty of such an attack.

5.   Discussion

Satisfaction of Goals

In order to ascertain the success, or otherwise, of the NELF design after integration with NGSCB, we can review the original security goals as defined in Table 1.

Goal $G1$, concerned with the integrity of a legal form, is assured with public key encryption. All legal forms are encrypted with the public key of their intended recipients before transmission. The goal is met for all concerned parties: the ADLS, and primary and secondary users. Integrity is assured through the cryptographic strength of the underlying encryption scheme.

Goal $G2$, concerned with the DRM-restricted availability of printing a legal form, is the most difficult to satisfy. As noted by the ADLS in their newsletter (Figure 3), every user of ELF is able to print, through the addition of the appropriate print driver, a legal form to PDF. As printing to PDF is unable to be prevented, it is important that the ADLS continue to inform primary users of the weaknesses of the PDF format.

Given the design described in this paper, which successfully reproduces the functionality given by using PDF — the ability to send legal documents to users with out an ELF installation — it is hoped that users will reduce their use of PDF. With increased use of the system outlined in this paper, with its high degree of confidentiality and integrity, it is hoped that any use of PDF to store or transport ADLS legal forms would be seen as malicious, or at the least, ill-informed. Given the legal community's noted [MM03] willingness to report firms or individuals using obviously unauthorised hard-copy forms, it is reasonable to assume the same would occur with PDF forms, especially once informed about the risks inherent in the PDF format. Goal $G2$ can only be met for the ADLS if primary users discontinue their use of PDF.

Goals $G3$ and $G4$ are met for both primary and secondary users. The PKI established during the administered enrolment of primary users enables those users to encrypt legal forms with the public keys of their intended recipients. The PKI described has a tightly controlled enrolment process, increasing trust in the identities of those enrolled. It serves a primary user's interests to keep their key pair secret as a third party can use it to create legal documents purporting to come from them. Should a key pair be compromised, revocation is handled at a central site by the ADLS. This PKI allows the method of legal form transmission as described in section 3, to continue to be used amongst primary users.

To meet $G3$ and $G4$ for transmission between primary and secondary users, a trust relationship is established between every secondary user with whom a primary user wishes to communicate. A primary user is then able to encrypt legal forms with the public key of the specific secondary user to whom they wish to transmit a legal form. Confidentiality is strictly enforced by the system, as the private key generated during the secondary user's NELF widget installation is never released outside the NGSCB platform by the NELF widget itself.

Shortcomings

To find and evaluate shortcomings, it is possible to evaluate the initial threats against the new architecture.

As noted in section 5, it is currently impossible to restrict the ability to file. Despite the ADLS being able to collect a single charge for any form printed to file, this file (in PDF, PS or PCL format) can then be used to generate any number of hard copies. It should be noted that once in any of these formats, threats $T2$ (creation of electronic template), $T3$ (modification of legalese) and $T4$ (modification of user-modifiable fields) cannot be mitigated. However, if the ADLS is successful in creating an aversion to using any format of electronic form transmission other than the NELF system described, these threats can be reduced. For example, all the noted threats from malicious third parties will be reduced, as they will not be able to obtain a copy of any legal form (guaranteed through attainment of the confidentiality goal). Without access to a copy, none of the denoted threats can occur from a third party.

The general problem of replay attacks outlined in section 2, causing threat $T1$ to occur from primary and secondary users, arises because the NGSCB platform has no form of persistent, secure storage. Discussions with Geoffrey Strongin, Platform Security Architect for Advanced Micro Devices [Str03] revealed that a working group has recently been set up within the Trusted Computing Group to develop trusted mass storage. Persistent storage that protects files stored by an NCA from modification or deletion, unless authorised by that same NCA, would enable a general solution to replay attacks.

Threats $T3$ and $T4$, described in section 3, are minimized as much as possible by using a public key encryption standard. If, as hoped, no legal form is ever released outside a primary user's NELF installation without encryption, $T3$ and $T4$ from malicious secondary users can be reduced.

It should be noted that the initial release of NGSCB would not allow NELF to secure printed output. Discussions with Microsoft security staff [CK03] indicated that improvements in this area are expected. Such secure printing will not come directly from Microsoft, but from other vendors in the printer marketplace. It is hoped that this will allow the restriction of printed output to a hard copy printer.

The NELF architecture proposed relies on NGSCB to be present on all systems in the distributed environment. How soon, if ever, that this will occur is a question that cannot be answered in this paper. As stated in the introduction, NGSCB is expected to make inroads in the corporate marketplace first. As such, the ability to secure high value legal documents could be one of the killer applications needed to drive NGSCB uptake.

6.   Conclusion

We have introduced Microsoft's NGSCB technology, and discussed it by way of a novel metaphor. It is hoped that this metaphor will be useful in explaining the concepts and architecture of NGSCB to those without a firm technical grasp of computer security. Trusted computing represents a fundamental shift in the way applications may operate, and it brings a number of dangers and benefits. It is imperative that consumers are able to make informed decisions about their use of the technology.

We have performed a detailed security analysis of an existing software application, and shown the source of a number of threats. After discussion with relevant parties, we have arrived at a number of security goals. A system architecture was then developed to meet these goals, through mitigation of the noted threats. We have shown it is possible to reduce various security threats to an existing application by way of integration with Microsoft's NGSCB.

Such integration illustrates that it is possible to redesign an existing application to make use of the new security primitives provided by NGSCB, without being forced to redesign completely, discarding the existing usability and strengths of an application.

Acknowledgments

The authors would like to gratefully acknowledge the assistance and willingness of the Auckland District Law Society, as well as correspondence received from various members of the NGSCB development team.

References

[ADL03]   ADLS. Auckland District Law Society. Available from http://www.adls.org.nz/, 2003.

[Bre01]   C T S Brendan. Protecting digital content within the home. *Computer*, 34(10):42–47, 2001.

[CK03]   Ellen Cram and Keith Kaplan.   Next-Generation Secure Computing Base - Overview and Drilldown. Presentation at Microsoft Professional Developers Conference, 27 Oct 2003.

[ELF03]   ELF. Electronic Legal Forms. Available from http://www.adls.org.nz/shop/elf.asp, 2003.

[ELMW03]   P. England, B. Lampson, J. Manferdelli, and B. Willman. A trusted open platform. *Computer*, 36(7):55–62, 2003.

[Gra03]   David Grawrock.   TPM main part 3 commands.   Available from https://www.trustedcomputinggroup.org/downloads/tpmwg-mainrev62_Part3_Commands.pdf, 2003.

[Mic03a]   Microsoft. *Hardware Platform for the Next-Generation Secure Comput-ing Base*, 2003. Available from http://www.microsoft.com/resources/NGSCB/documents/NGSCBhardware.doc.

[Mic03b]   Microsoft. *NGSCB Product Information*, 2003. Available from http://www.microsoft.com/resources/NGSCB/productinfo.mspx.

[Mic03c]   Microsoft. *NGSCB: Trusted Computing Base and Software Authentication*, 2003. Available from http://www.microsoft.com/resources/NGSCB/documents/NGSCB_tcb.doc.

[Mic03d]   Microsoft. *Security Model for the Next-Generation Secure Computing Base*, 2003. Available from http://www.microsoft.com/resources/NGSCB/documents/NGSCB_Security_Model.doc.

[MM03]   Marcus Martin and Simon Marsden. Meeting, 14 Aug 2003.

[MP01]   Antonio Mana and Ernesto Pimentel. An efficient software protection scheme. In *Proceedings of the 16th international conference on Information security: Trusted information*, pages 385–401. 2001. Paris, France.

[Pfl97]   C. Pfleeger. Is there a security problem in computing? In *Security in Computing*, pages 1–19. Prentice Hall, 2nd edition edition, 1997.

[RC03]   Kenneth Ray and Ellen Cram. Interview at Microsoft Professional Developers Conference, 29 Oct 2003.

[Spi03]   Domidis Spinellis. Reflections on trusting trust revisited. *Communications of the ACM*, 46(6):112, 2003.

[Sta02]   Richard Stallman. Can you trust your computer? Available from http://www.gnu.org/philosophy/can-you-trust.html, 2002.

[Str03]   Geoffrey Strongin. Platform Security Architect, Advanced Micro Devices. Inter-view at Microft Professional Developers Conference, 28 Oct 2003.

[TCG03a]   TCG.   Trusted Computing Group.   Available from http://www.trustedcomputinggroup.org/home, 2003.

[TCG03b]   TCG.   Trusted Platform Module main specification.   Available from   https://www.trustedcomputinggroup.org/downloads/tpmwg-mainrev62_Part3_C%ommands.pdf, Dec 2003.

USE OF ELECTRONIC IDENTITY CARDS IN THE PRIVATE SECTOR

Lionel Khalil

LIPN, Institut Galilée, Université Paris 13
99 av. J-B. Clément, 93430 Villetaneuse, France
lionel.khalil@lipn.univ-paris13.fr

Abstract   Based on the evaluation of real-life application experiences, we have proposed a definition of Trust- and Quality-based Risk analysis to better understand the user's judgement; we have emphasized that the e-government should be driving the development of the use of ID-cards in the private sector. We have tried to propose basic concepts to urbanise the development of ID-cards: people may accept the constraints of in-depth authentication only in relation to trusted Institutions. Applications of this technology must be limited and separated into categories of equal risk and frequency of use.

Keywords: risk analysis, identity cards, trust

1.   Introduction

Banks and other Institutions are currently using paper-based ID-Cards and signatures in their services; so, banks are involved in the development of Electronic Identity Card (ID-card) models. In the past, numerous online payment methods have been devised and their implementation has constituted very instructive but fruitless attempts to transpose and make less visible traditional banking techniques, originally developed with the use of practical media [Bou04]. Whatever their benefits and performance may be like, their deployment has appeared prohibitive faced with competition from less secure systems constituted by the transmission "in mid air" of a bank card number.

Let's define trust as a perception of security and a presupposition of the quality of the Institution. When people talk about authentication in e-technology, they talk as if their only concern is risk management, regardless of the client's perception of trust. The existence of the transaction is based on trust through the authentication of both sides. On the application side, the validation of the commitment of the client's side is rationally based on risk analysis and risk management with regard to the security of the system. On the client side, the validation of the commitment of the application's side is based on trust. Thus, the issue of trust is fundamental to the success of e-commerce.

Based on the real-life application experiences of bank and governmental projects, we want to express methodological proposals for organizational issues in implementing ID-cards' urbanisation in a multilateral context regarding the protection and social implications of ID-Cards, such as users' security responsibilities and protection of users' privacy.

In this paper we consider that private sector needs in many cases to identify their clients. Before, they were using the paper based Identity Card. Because of the evolution of the e-government, the private sector should remain involved in the creation of Electronic Identity Card (ID-card) models [Kha03a]. We present two main points to this approach. We consider that the e-government has to lead the development of Electronic Identity Cards or e-ID card, not only for the access to e-government services, but also to be used for business transactions in the private sector. This approach points out that applications of this technology must be separated into categories of equal risk and frequency of use. This makes this approach a good strategy for the implementation of Electronic Identity Cards.

Overview. The rest of this paper is structured as follows: In section 2 we will present a definition of Quality-based Risk analysis. Section 3 motivates the work by showing examples in Europe of the kind of system we would like to model: in some projects the ID-card is only used for access to e-government services. The France case study gives an alternative view, where the private and public sectors share the use of ID-card. Then we would like to argue two points with regard to this subject. In section 4 we formalise the idea that the e-government should be leading the development of the use of ID-cards in the private sector. Section 5 describes why applications of this technology must be limited and separated into categories of equal risk and frequency of use. Finally, we conclude the paper in section 6.

2.   Definition of Quality-based Risk Analysis

We remind you of the definition of Risk Management approved by A.N.S.I. [ATIS01]: "The process concerned with identification, measurement, control and minimisation of security risks in information systems to a level commensurate with the value of the assets protected". On the Institution side, the risk assessment is based on a process of analyzing exposure to risk and determining how to best handle such exposure.

Banking experts are using classical risk analysis: the market needs an in-depth authentication payment system with physical use of the card. In the past, there have been fruitless attempts to impose in-depth authentication in e-commerce. The judgement of the market was severe: no added value for high security payment systems. We think that the risk analysis from the user's view point is different from the bank's view point.

Regardless of the interest of the transaction between a client and an Institution, the evaluation of the risk of the transaction is different for each side because the environments of each side are different. On the Institution side, the risk is evaluated by a process of risk management analysis, and on the client side, the risk is mainly an evaluation based on a quality-based risk analysis.

To define a quality-based risk analysis, we need to define the notion of trust.

In [Men01], Mendez et al. propose the definition of trust developed by Lorentz in [Lor82, Lor01], which provides the following definition: trust is a bounded rational analysis which evaluates an expectation of goodwill and benign intent. This analysis is an anticipation of the behavior for a specific task based on a generalization of normalized behavior for a similar task.

There are 4 segmentations of this analysis :

- assurance - incentive structure,

- commitment (long term relationship),

- familiarity,

- and representation.

Trust is re-evaluated in real-time with new information. A similar definition was expressed in [Kar96] by Karpik. Trust is composed of inductive, calculated, and normative judgements based on an interaction process between respectively emotional, intellectual, and social commitments (see also [Noo01]):

- inductive judgements based on emotional commitments,

- calculated judgements based on intellectual commitments,

- and normative judgements based on social commitments.

Classical risk analysis: a rational analysis is to minimise the exposure to risk based on the evaluation of the damaged and trust is analyzed as a weakness.

without trust, risk is infinite - social judgement is embedded in the risk analysis and trust is a necessary asset to evaluate the risk analysis.

Remark: there is a difference between integrating organizational issues in an evaluation scheme as an asset (for example Human Machine Interaction and social engineering evaluation) and the fact that the system itself is based on trust.

For example, a CA in a PKI is trusted because the Institution that owns the CA is trusted. This trust is mainly outside the scope of the evaluation of the classical risk analysis of the organisation of the PKI.

With this definition, we can precisely define the commitment of both sides in a transaction: on the application's side, commitment is rationally based on classical risk analysis and risk management, and the commitment on the user's side remains how to best handle the risk's exposure, based on a quality-based risk analysis.

On the client's side, the Institution's risk analysis remains both a perception of security and a presupposition of the quality of the Institution. We refer to [Men01, Kar98, Wil93] for a detailed demonstration that Concludes that a transaction is based on an evaluation of "why we conclude a transaction"; and trust and risk management are based on "how we conclude a transaction".

The perception of ID-cards issued by Institutions (such as the government, notaries, banks, the post) is based on a quality-based risk analysis. The evaluation of trust changes with time: in the short term perception, Trust is linked to the Institution; in the medium- term the user re-evaluates the risk through the everyday use of the e-card. The risk management evaluation has to reinforce the trust [Kha03b].

3.   Overview in Europe and case study in France

Many member states of the EU (European Union) are currently evaluating the introduction of e-ID cards or have already started deployment. The Electronic Identity Card supports different names: Electronic Identity Card in Italy for example [AFNT04, ACFN⁺04], ID-Card in Finland, Electronic Identity Card for Belgian Citizens or e-ID for Maltese citizens. These cards are the electronic version of the current National identity card that enables secure access to and use of the e-government services. Two main projects are supported by the European Community: EUCLID and eEpoch [eEpoch01]. EUCLID (European initiative for a Citizen digital ID solution) is a project funded by the European Community under the Information Society Technology programme. It responded to the identified needs of the citizens and the business community by improving the security of transactions and interoperability of the cards. eEpoch is a Demonstration Project of the Information Society Technologies Programme of the European Union and it is organized according to the framework defined by the European Commission. The aim of eEpoch is to demonstrate interoperable and secure smart card based digital identification systems, which provide the levels of trust and confidence necessary for citizens to interact digitally with their national and local authorities and other European institutions [San04].

In some countries the e-government has decided to lead the development of Electronic Identity Cards or e-ID card, not only for access to e-government services, but also to be used for business transactions in the private sector. The Italian project goes further in interoperability between private and public services: the Electronic Identity Card includes a National Multiservice Card. In the UK, the NERSC (North East Regional Smartcard Consortium) is a region-wide multi-application citizen smartcard that can be used for travel throughout the North East Region to support local authority public services as well as other commercial applications [NERSC03]. In [Eng02], Engel recalls that the legal issues in relation to the use of public ID in the private sector have already been addressed by the EU.

The French experience is an example of the privatisation of ID-card issu-ing. For 4 years, the French banks were working on two parallel projects: the Identrus network and Ministry of Finance Certificates (MINEFI). The first one was a worldwide project. But French banks did not find an ideal applica-tion for an Identrus Certificate. Therefore the Banks decided not to implement the Identrus infrastructure, but to buy on demand Identrus Certificates (from other Identrus Banks) and brand and resell these certificates to end-users. This position is a defensive position with regard to the development of Identrus Certificates: the major expected benefits of this solution are the short time-to-market and low initial investments. The main concern of the Banks was to control the customer's commercial relationship. Meanwhile, there was coop-eration between the financial industry and the Ministry of Finance to agree on common standards for electronic signatures in the e-government and e-banking (except that Identrus certificates are not compliant with MINEFI certificates), with one target being that bank signatures will be used for the e-government, hence enabling government to save on costs [Kha02]. The Ministry of Finance pushed for soft certificates for the e-government three years ago, and banks issued around 30,000 to companies for VAT and social taxes; each year extra services have been added. These may also be used for corporate on-line bank-ing. Although the Ministry of Finance has been pressing banks to issue its certificates, the Ministry of the Interior wants now to issue its own certificates. Even though this cooperation was a success, the privatisation of ID-cards is-sued for corporations was not accepted in all branches of government, mainly because the project was held by the Ministry of Finance while the Ministry of the Interior was historically in charge of Electronic Identity Cards. Today, the Ministry of the Interior is trying to take over the project from the Ministry of Finance. One of the main subjects of disagreement lies in the privatisation of Electronic Identity Card issuing. But the new project to reissue Electronic Identity Cards for corporations and small and medium enterprizes will face two problems: the disagreement of banks who have already invested in the project of their supervisory Ministry, and the current lack of budget from the government. Unfortunately, this situation sends unclear messages to the mar-ket and reduces trust in e-government policy. The weaknesses of the project were clear: no interoperability between ID-Cards for corporate on-line bank-ing. Banks remain in competition and those certificates are rejected by other

Ministries. Nevertheless, the e-government should be leading the development of Electronic Identity Cards and sending clear messages to the market.

4.   The e-government should be leading the development of ID-technology.

In real life, business partners and customers do not need an in-depth authentication of their partners. There are two exceptions: bill payments and credit services for Banks, and government taxes and official documents. The law admits the validity of contracts even when partners do not know each other well (see [Kha02]). After the Internet Revolution, each government decided to offer on-line services. But the problem with in-depth authentication remains the same as in real life. The whole economy, meanwhile, has been working on-line without in-depth authentication. ID-cards are a concern for banks and the government and one of them has to create the market. If Electronic Identity Cards are privatized the following problems may arise: banks remain in competition, as, even though they are taking a State role, they will prefer to promote their own branded Electronic Identity Card which is linked with their own products and services, even in an interoperable model. The privatisation of ID-cards is too sensitive an issue. The e-government has to mandate the interoperability of private Electronic Identity Cards in order to fulfil the needs of the Corporations and Small and Medium Enterprizes market. The main question is: under what conditions will the whole market accept an all-in-one card? Some elements of the answer lie in the notions of protection of the right to privacy and liberty, added value, and risk management. If banks have to develop an e-card project, the banks should follow the lead of government policy and priorities. One of the reasons is that the market needs a clear separation of powers.

5.   The market needs a clear separation of powers.

People accept to transfer some of their power in their ID-tokens. People do not make the distinction between authentication and authorization; so while a token can give access to its holder to many services, the risk to the holder is the sum of the risk of each service. The perception of the token is both positive and negative: positive because it opens up many services and negative because the holder has to protect it. For example, in the US, with a Social Security Number and a birth certificate one can get a passport, a driving licence and a bank account. In this section, we propose basic concepts to urbanise the development of ID-cards to respect users' needs, users' protection and a multilateral context.

Urbanisation constraints of users' needs are a direct relationship between facility of use, frequency of use and risk. The holder's protectiveness towards the token is higher when the power given is higher, and is higher when activation of the card is easier. "People don't want to pull out their passport each time they need to buy groceries." Different kinds of services require different levels of power transferred. The perception of the added values and risks of carrying an ID-card depend on the level of power which is transferred in this ID-Card. Thus, only ID-Cards with the same value and the same frequency of use can be merged.

Urbanisation constraints to respect users' protection become stronger. Due to people's desire to defend a strong sense of liberty, they prefer to separate different aspects of their lives. People are sensitive to the protection of their right to privacy. Even though the service might say that it is only accessing a specific aspect or part of a multi-application, people won't trust it. People do not want to use their private ID-Cards in a professional situation. Their cautiousness reflects their reluctance to mix different aspects of their lives. The protection of privacy pushes towards separate identifiers for different activities in life: professional badges, personal Security Social Number, personal ID-card and personal driving licence.

In addition, if people lose an all-in-one ID, they have no other ID to fall back on. All services would be blocked. More than one card would avoid access to public services being denied.

Urbanisation constraints will manage organizational security in a multilateral context. Current risks will be amplified. Urbanisation has to manage the order to obtain different cards: no opportunity for a procedure allowing the creation from scratch of a false ID. In a multilateral context, do not create an all-in-one pass card which will attract criminal interest.

A potential solution would be to have more than one card: one for everyday life and one for more sensitive information. The characteristic of the everyday life card would be to benefit from quick issuing, and services with a high frequency of use and low risk in the transaction, such as some administrative services, transport services, public leisure services, student ID, library access, canteen pass, or electronic purse. On the other hand, for the second more classic ID-card, we can imagine in-depth control upon issuing. All the e-government services including a full recognized electronic signature like a traditional paper-based ID-card. Depending on the country the driving licence and the Social Security Card could be separated or merged with one of these two cards.

Thus the development of private ID-Cards has no hope outside the policy of an ID-Card launched by the government. The private sector will take advantage of remaining close to the e-government standards. We will leave the case study of the difficulty of embedded applications between banks and government for future work.

6.   Conclusion

We have shown that several interesting projects have been launched within a precise framework. Based on the evaluation of real-life application experiences, we have proposed a definition of Trust and Quality-based Risk analysis to better understand users' judgement; we have emphasized that the e-government should be driving the development of the use of ID-cards in the private sector. We have tried to propose basic concepts to urbanise the development of ID-cards: people may accept the constraints of in-depth authentication only in relation to trusted Institutions. Due to people's desire to defend a strong sense of liberty, they prefer to separate different aspects of their lives.

We emphasize specifically the role of applications with the same level of risk and use. E-society could not propose today a unique card for all services: to protect privacy, to avoid denied access for people who lose the card, and not to attract the interest of criminals.

The all-in-one Card can only be developed by Institutions which have the same interests, which are not in competition, or which are their clients' only providers, Institutions which have their clients' trust, such as governmental institutions, schools, public transport companies, and, in many cases, banks. People may accept the constraints of in-depth authentication only in relation to these Institutions.

A pragmatic solution would be to develop at least two ID-cards, one for everyday life and one to replace the paper-based National Identity Card. The private sector needs to integrate the use of these ID-cards into its e-commerce strategy.

References

[AFNT04] Franco Arcieri, Fabio Fioravanti, Enrico Nardelli, Maurizio Talamo. Reliable peer-to-peer access for Italian citizens to digital government services on the Internet. 3rd International Conference on Electronic Government (EGOV-04) Zaragoza, Spain, Aug.2004. In *Lecture Notes in Computer Science*, vol.3183

[ACFN+04] Franco Arcieri, Mario Ciclosi, Fabio Fioravanti, Enrico Nardelli, Maurizio Talamo. The Italian Electronic Identity Card: a short introduction. 5th U.S. National Conference on Digital Government (DGO-04) Seattle, Wa., USA, May.04. http://www.diggov.org/library/library/dgo2004/

[ATIS01] Alliance for Telecommunications Industry Solutions. Telecom Glossary 2000. approved by American National Standards Institute, Inc. T1.523-2001, February 28, 2001.

[Bou04] D. Bounie and P. Gazé. Payment and Internet: Analysis, Stakes and Research Perspectives in Economics of Banking, May 2004.

[eEpoch01] eEpoch. e-ID and the Information Society in Europe. White Paper, september 2001.

[Eng02] S. Engel-Flechsig. Study on legal issues in relation to the use of public ID (Electronic Identity) Radicchio Ltd. UK, October 2002.

[Kar96] L. Karpik. Dispositifs de confiance et engagements crédibles. *Sociol. Trav.* num 4, 527-550, 1996.

[Kar98] L. Karpik. La confiance: réalité ou illusion? Examen critique d'une thèse de Williamson. *Rev. Eco.* vol. 49, num 4, 1043-1056, 1998.

[Kha03a] L. Khalil. Signature électronique: certificats qualifiés "publics" ou certificats qualifiés "privés". In *Communication et commerce électronique*, num 4. page 11, avril 2003.

[Kha03b] L. Khalil. Enjeux de l'acte authentique électronique. In *Colloque sur l'Acte authentique du 17-18 octobre 2003 - Université de La Rochelle*, Droit In Situ éd. , 2003.

[Kha02] L. Khalil. *Signature électronique: le cadre juridique d'une autorité de certification bancaire.* Thèse, ANRT ed., 2002.

[Lor01] E. Lorentz. Inter-organizational trust, boundary spanners and communities of practice. In *Réseaux.* num 108, 65-85, FT R&D Hermès Science Publication, 2001.

[Lor82] E. Lorentz. Confiance, contrats et coopération économique. *Sociol. Trav.* num 4, 487-508, 1982.

[Men01] A. Mendez, N.Richez-Battesti. Pour une vision dynamique de la confiance: quelques réflexions à partir d'une banque mutualiste. In *Confiance et rationalité*, Dijon, 5-6 May 1999. In Les colloques, num 97, Ed INRA, Paris, 2001.

[Noo01] B. Nooteboom. How to combine calculative and non-calculative trust. In *Trust and Trouble in organizations.* Symposium , Erasmus University, Rotterdam, May, 2001.

[NERSC03] North East Regional Smartcard Consortium. *The North East A Community of Communitie*, 2003.

[San04] R. Sanchez-Reillo. *Pan-European interoperability solutions: Experiences from eEpoch Pilot Sites.* 2004, e-ID Workshop on e-Go for reliable e-services: Electronic Identity from theory to practice, 2004.

[Wil93] O.E. Williamson. Calculativeness, Trust and Economic Organization. *J. Law Econ.*, volume XXXVI, April, 453-487, 1993.

BUSINESS RISK MANAGEMENT BASED ON A SERVICE PORTFOLIO APPROACH FOR AN EQUIPMENT-PROVIDING SERVICE

Tadasuke Nakagawa[1], Shigeyuki Tani[1],
Chizuko Yasunobu[1] and Norihisa Komoda[2]

[1]*Hitachi, Ltd., Systems Development Laboratory, Hitachi System Plaza Shinkawasaki, 890, Kashimada, Saiwai-ku, Kawasaki-shi, Kanagawa- ken, 212-8567 Japan*

[2]*Osaka University, 2-1, Yamadaoka, Suita- shi, Osaka-fu, 565-0871 Japan*

Abstract   In recent years, companies have become reluctant to accept the risk associated with investment in equipment. Therefore, equipment-providing services, where an outside provider owns the equipment and collects fees for its use from the user, have become increasingly popular because they reduce the users' investment risks. In exchange for receiving these fees, an equipment provider takes on part of each user's operating risk. For such a service to be profitable, though, the supplier must be able to accurately determine the appropriate risk and measure how much of this risk it is accepting instead of the user. It is critical that the equipment provider have an effective means to control the risk and understand its potential negative effect.

Keywords: equipment-providing services; risk; price

1.   Introduction

In recent years, the uncertainty surrounding corporate management has risen for several reasons, and investment in an enterprise and equipment is increasingly risky in terms of future profitability. As a result, many businesses now prefer to keep such investment at arm's length by obtaining equipment through equipment-providing services. In this service, an equipment provider makes the initial investment, and the provider's profits depend on how each user operates the equipment. In this way, the provider also takes on some of the user's operating risk. For an equipment provider to operate profitably, it must be able to accurately determine the amount of risk related to such equipment provision and price its services accordingly. To enable this, we have developed a profitability simulator for equipment-providing services . Conventionally, con-

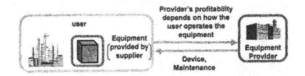

Figure 1.   Business Model of an Equipment-providing Service

tracts have been priced according to the amount of risk associated with each contract, and it has been assumed that although a provider and user can share the operating risk this risk cannot be decreased.

In this research, we show that equipment-providers can reduce their overall risk through diversification since they serve users in various types of industry and different regions of operation. Since diversification reduces the overall risk, an equipment provider can offer such a service at a lower price which reflects the risk reduction made possible by a portfolio approach rather than taking an individual-contract perspective.

The rest of this paper is organized as follows. Chapter 2 describes the risk-management method conventionally used by an equipment-providing service and the problem with this method. In Chapter 3, we explain the portfolio effect and how it should be reflected in service pricing. In Chapter 4, we validate the effectiveness of this approach. We conclude in Chapter 5.

2.   Business Risk Management for Equipment-Providing Services

Business Risk Management on a Contract Basis

The business model of equipment-providing services, where an equipment-provider rather than a user owns the equipment, is outlined in Figure 1. Equipment-providers supply various types of equipment such as information technology (IT) hardware or energy-saving equipment and charge a fee which depends on, for example, the amount of equipment used, the usage time, or the effect. However, since the provider's profitability depends on how the user operates the equipment, an important characteristic of an equipment-providing service is that the user and the equipment provider share the uncertainty (risk) regarding future returns on investment. For an equipment provider to avoid taking on excessive risk and ensure long-term profitability, the provider must accurately determine the amount of risk it accepts for each service offer and price the offer accordingly. Our approach to this problem is to consider first the risk with regard to fluctuations. To accurately determine the amount of risk, we develop an equipment-provider profit simulator. And, we use the size of the profit-prediction range to define the amount of risk.

Problem with Conventional Methods

The methods conventionally used have a certain limitation, as follows.

1 An equipment provider typically has service contracts with many users, and the number of risks which a service supplier is exposed to will expand as the number of users rises. To run such a service safely, the provider must be able to determine the total amount of risk.

2 Conventionally, a provider prices such a service by determining the potential costs of the risks associated with each service contract assuming that these risks are shared between the user and the provider and that the amount of inherent risk cannot be reduced.

3.   Risk Management through a Service Portfolio Approach

Quantification of the Service Portfolio Effect

When the total risk taken on by an equipment provider is conventionally calculated, the overall risk is considered to be a simple sum of the amount of risk associated with each service contract. In this research, we quantify the total amount of risk based on portfolio theory. A portfolio is a combination of various assets owned by an investor. By combining assets with different risk characteristics with regard to profitability, portfolio investment allows an investor to reduce risk through diversification. An equipment provider holds a portfolio of service contracts, and each contract can be considered an asset. We think that the risk associated with each contract can be reduced by combining many contracts whose profitability will depend on different factors, such as industry type and region of operations. The amount of risk reduction achieved through such diversification can be quantified.

The overall risk of a portfolio is computed using the variance and covariance of the returns generated by the contracts held in the portfolio. In this way, a linear relationship between the portfolio return and effective risk assessment can be established. The standard deviation $S(R_p)$ is expressed (1) where R_p is portfolio, γ_i is the investment rate of asset i, σ_{ii} denotes the variance of the return from asset i, and σ_{ij} denotes the covariance between the returns of asset i and asset j.

$$S(R_p) = \sqrt{\sum_i \sum_j \gamma_i \gamma_j \sigma_{ij}} \tag{1}$$

As for investment in stocks, Eq. (1) is used when asset is distributed to each brand. However, since the service itself can not be distributed in an equipment-providing service, we can assume that $\gamma = 1 (i = 1, 2, ..., N)$. That is, $S(R_p)$ is expressed as

$$S(R_p) = \sqrt{\sum_i \sum_j \sigma_{ij}} \tag{2}$$

The amount of risk is defined using $S(R_p)$ of Eq. (2). In this research, using an arbitrary constant a , we define the amount of risk Q using the standard deviation $S(R_p)$ of a portfolio as

$$Q = aS(R_p) \tag{3}$$

Constant a can be determined using a value at risk (VaR) approach. VaR is a risk index which shows the maximum amount of a potential loss as statistically determined for a fixed confidence interval when financial assets are held for a fixed period. If we assume that the returns from each contract follow a normal distribution for an equipment-providing service, and the period of possession is fixed, constant a can be determined by setting up a confidence interval. An equipment provider should ensure that the amount of risk Q associated with that contract does not exceed the permitted amount of potential loss.

Pricing on a Portfolio Basis

Because of diversification, the total risk is less than the simple sum of the risk of each contract. Denoting the standard deviation of the return of each contract as σ_i, we can express the effectiveness of diversified investment as

$$S(R_p) \leq \sum_i \sigma_i \tag{4}$$

Given the lower risk that the provider is exposed to, the pricing of a contract can be reduced. By accurately calculating the risk, we can determine the minimum value of, for example, a service contract.

Our proposed pricing method and the conventional pricing method are compared in Figure 2. In the past each risk premium was based on the risk of the contract, and the price was determined by adding an appropriate risk premium to the cost of providing the service. However, since the total risk that an equipment provider is exposed to depends also on the effect of diversification, each contract price can reflect the saving achieved through diversification. When the risk associated with a contract is expressed as $a_i \sigma_i$ using the arbitrary constants a_i and standard deviation σ_i, the risk premium $P(i)$ for service i is expressed by the following formula based on the amount of portfolio risk Q.

$$P(i) = Q \frac{a_i \sigma_i}{\sum a_i \sigma_i} \tag{5}$$

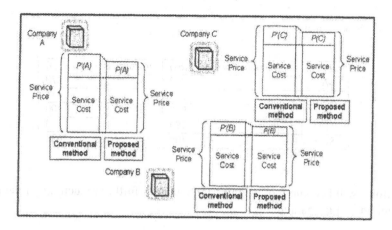

Figure 2. Service Price

Here, to take into account the amount of risk for each contract, $P(i)$ is calculated based on a proportional division of the sum total of risk from all contracts. A lower service price can be offered during contract negotiation based on this $P(i)$.

4. Verification

We offer our clients one example of the equipment-providing service. We applied our proposed approach based on a simulation using the charge data from our service to verify the validity of this approach. $P(i)$ was computed using data from the actual service period. The charge data used for verification (Figure 3) was obtained from four services over seven months. The calculated monthly risk premium $P'(i) = a_i\sigma_i$ and $P(i)$ are compared in Table 1.

We obtained $\sum a_i\sigma_i = 2,106$ and $Q = 1,638$. The proposed method thus reduced the conventional risk premium by 22.2%, showing that this approach justifies reducing the contract price. We expect the number of services to increase in the future. Therefore, the effect of diversification within the service

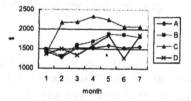

Figure 3. Charge Data

Table 1. Risk Premium

service	conventional method ($a_i\sigma_i$)	proposed method ($P(i)$)
A	347	270
B	563	438
C	900	700
D	296	230
Sum	2106	1638

portfolio will become more significant, enabling further reductions in the risk premium that is charged.

5. Conclusion

Summary

We have shown that an equipment provider can reduce its share of operating risk by providing services to many users in various industries and regions of operation through diversification. By taking an approach where each equipment provider is assumed to hold a portfolio of contracts, we have shown how the total risk a provider is exposed to can be computed. Moreover, we have shown how the pricing of a service contract can be lowered by taking into account the risk reduction achieved through a diversified portfolio approach. We have verified the validity of this approach by simulating its application based on data from the equipment-providing service provided by our company.

Future study

If the returns from new services are weakly or negatively correlated with those from current services, further reduction in the portfolio risk will be possible. Although the present risk premium in contract pricing reflects a proportional division of the risk taken on by the provider, taking into consideration the correlation between the returns from each service and those from other services will enable more suitable pricing with regard to overall risk. In the future, we will work towards developing specific methods for doing this.

References

[WB99] R. Wise and P. Baumgartner, "Go Downstream: The New Profit Imperative in Manufacturing," Harvard Business Review, Vol. 77, no. 5, pp. 133-141, 1999.

[Ben89] S. Benninga, *NUMERICAL TECHNIQUE IN FINANCE.* (MIT Press, 1989).

[GS01] G. Grimmett and D. Stirzaker, *Probability and Random Processes.* (Third ed., Oxford University Press, 2001).

A WEB SERVICE FOR CERTIFIED EMAIL

Vincenzo Auletta, Carlo Blundo, Stelvio Cimato and Guerriero Raimato
Dipartimento di Informatica ed Applicazioni
Università di Salerno
84100 Baronissi (Salerno), Italy
{auletta, carblu, cimato, raimato}@dia.unisa.it

Keywords: Security Protocol, Certified Email.

Abstract   Web service technology allows the completion of complex tasks through the definition of simpler collaborating services. As soon as Web services become available a challenging problem is the provision of means by which the data exchange and the service usage can be proofed. An interesting test case comes from the development of Web based certified email systems. In such systems users exchanging email messages would like to get some additional guarantees on the security of the communication during the interaction. In this work we describe the design and the implementation of a certified email application realized through the definition of interacting servers. Users access the service through a Web based application and are able to get, at the end of the transaction, a valid receipt which can be used in case of dispute.

1.   Introduction

Web service technology is changing the way complex distributed applications are being developed. Indeed, such an approach offers a comprehensive set of platform-independent technologies and open standards which have been released in order to ease the delivery of new services over the Internet. Many companies are investing large amount of money in research and development projects related to the exploitation of such kind of technologies, expecting a number of technical and economical benefits [CCS03].

One of the key feature of Web service technology is the "loose coupling" paradigm which favors the integrations of interacting applications within a company or between different companies. By adopting such new development model, time and cost savings can be obtained by the use of standard interfaces and the reuse of existing applications. In addition, complex tasks can be achieved by the composition of simpler collaborating services. Instead of developing static applications, new business services can be defined out of available services, providing the flexibility needed to respond to rapidly changing customer and market requirements.

In order to support the creation of higher level and cross-organizational business processes, several proposals have been made to define extensions to the Web services standard framework. The terms *orchestration* and *choreography* of Web services usually refer to the set of emerging specifications dealing with the combination and collaboration of Web services for the creation of composite business processes. Microsoft's XLANG [Tha01], IBM's WSFL [Ley01], BPEL4WS [CGKL+02] (by a consortium grouping Microsoft, IBM, BEA; SAP and other companies) are some of the currently available initiatives addressing some of the orchestration issues.

As soon as companies provide business services and release new Web services enabled products and tools, security becomes an increasing concern. Indeed, Web services applications let the information flow overcome the traditional boundaries between different companies, exposing data and internal structures to external potentially malicious users. Furthermore, Web service transactions span multiple applications and organizations, complicating the way access control policies can be setup or the tracking and the response to an attack can be done. In such scenario, it is important to provide security mechanisms which can be used during the data exchange in order to guarantee some basic security properties, stating for example the origin of a message (authentication), the destination of the message (authorization), the protection of the content of the message from modifications (integrity) and unauthorized access (confidentiality). [Bro03]

An interesting application useful to illustrate how some of the above security properties can be achieved in the development of a Web service is a certified email system. A certified email service tries to provide users with additional guarantees on the content and the delivery of the email messages, with respect to the ordinary email service. Indeed the standard e-mail service is based on the Simple Mail Transfer Protocol which offers no guarantees on the delivery and the authenticity of the messages, neither gives to the sender any evidence on the sending as well as any return receipt. A transmitted message could be eavesdropped over its path from the origin to the destination, and its content could be manipulated or corrupted by any malicious adversary. In literature, several distributed protocols for certified email have been proposed, relying on a trusted third party (TTP) to ensure the fairness of the protocol.

In this paper we describe a certified mail service based on the protocol described in [AHGP02]. The system is realized through the interaction of three main entities: the Webmail server for the sender, the Webmail server for the receiver and a Trusted Third Party. At the end of the transaction, the sender is able to get a receipt which can be shown in case of dispute. We discuss the details of the protocol in Section 3, and the basic security properties guaranteed by the proposed system in Section 6.

2.   Certified Email Protocols

Certified email protocols ensure that a participant exchanges a message for a receipt, which the receiver should release at the end of the transaction. Indeed, the aim of such protocols is to provide a procedure for the secure exchange of messages which is resistant to possible attempts of cheating by the different participants. Certified email protocols can be seen as instances of fair exchange protocols [ASW98] which guarantee the fair exchange of objects, i.e., at the end of the exchange, both participants get what they expect or nobody gets any valuable information.

Recently a lot of research has been dedicated to the problem of designing certified email protocols that satisfy the above properties. Several protocols involve a trusted third party (TTP for short) which is delegated by the participants to control the behavior of the parties, assist them during the exchange of messages, and resolve any dispute if necessary. According to the role played by the TTP, protocols have been classified as *inline* or *optimistic*. In inline protocols [BT94, GZ96, DGLW96, RS98], the TTP is actively involved in each message exchange: both the parties send their messages to the TTP , which checks for their integrity and forwards them to the intended receiver. In optimistic protocols [ASW97, ASW98], the sender and the receiver first try to exchange the message by themselves, without the intervention of the TTP and rely on the TTP only for the cases where a dispute arises (maybe because one of the party is trying to cheat). Protocols that do not require a trusted third party have also been proposed [Blu83, EGL85]. The main drawback of these protocols is that they require a large number of exchanges between the parties.

3.   The Framework

The scenario we consider consists of a number of users which are willing to exchange e-mail messages using a certified mail service. The service provides them with some additional guarantees on the delivery of the messages and on the security of the communication. To such purpose, the protocol relies on a Trusted Third Party (TTP) actively involved in each message exchange.

In the following we describe the cryptographic primitives used in the protocol: $Sig_A(m)$ denotes the digital signature of the message m using the private key of user A under a public-key signature algorithm; $h(m)$ indicates the hash of message m using some collision resistant hashing scheme. A collision resistant hash function maps arbitrary length messages to constant size messages such that it is computationally infeasible to find any two distinct messages hashing to the same value; $PK_B(m)$ denotes the encryption of message m

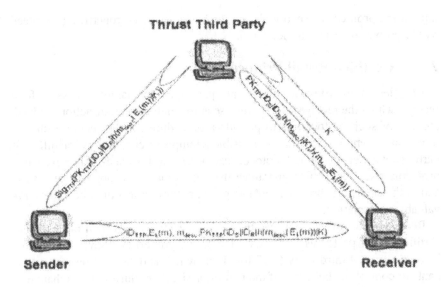

Figure 1. The protocol

using the public key of user B in some public-key encryption algorithm. The algorithm should provide non-malleability, i.e., given a ciphertext it is impossible to generate another ciphertext such that the respective plaintexts are related; $E_k(m)$ denotes the encryption of message m using the key k under some symmetric encryption algorithm.

Description of the Protocol

In this section we briefly recall the protocol presented by Abadi et al in [AHGP02], whose sketch is presented in Figure 1. The goal of the protocol is to allow a sender S to send an email message to a receiver R, in such a way that R reads the message if and only if S receives a valid return receipt. Other properties discussed in Section 2 are satisfied. Some of these properties derive from the use of cryptographic primitives, others derive directly from the protocol.

1 When S wants to send an email message m with subject s to R, he chooses a session key k and encrypts the message m using k obtaining $E_k(m)$. Afterwards, he adds a brief description m_{desc} of the message m and computes the hash $h(m_{desc}||E_k(m))$. S should also compute and store the $S2TTP$, which is the encryption under the public key of the TTPof the receiver identifier, the sender identifier, the key k associated with the message and the hash previously computed, i.e.,

$S2TTP = PK_{TTP}(ID_R, ID_S, k, h(m_{desc}||E_k(m)))$. The message sent to R consists of the TTP identifier, which R can contact to read the email message, the encrypted message $E_k(m)$, the message description in cleartext m_{desc}, and the string $S2TTP$.

2 On the reception of the message, R can read the description of the message and decide whether he wants to get the content of the email message from S. If he does, he forwards to the TTP (whose address is contained in the received message) the $S2TTP$ together with the hash $h(m_{desc}||E_k(m))$ containing the message description and the encrypted message. Otherwise, if R is not interested in the message, he can simply ignore the message and abort the protocol.

3 Whenever the TTP receives the message from R, he can decrypt $S2TTP$ and retrieve the key k and the hash $h'(m_{desc}|E_k(m))$. He then verifies that $h'(m_{desc}|E_k(m))$ matches with the hash received from R and in this case forwards the key k to R in order to let him read the mail, and sends S the signed receipt $Sig_{TTP}(S2TTP)$, which S can show as proof of the email sending.

4. The Architecture of the Certified Email Service

In this section we describe an architecture to implement the Web service based certified email system. Our system relies on three main entities interacting with the client and the receiver applications. Such components expose the services needed to realize all the phases of the protocol:

- **Sender's Webmail Server** (WMS_S): The WMS_S exposes two services: *Send* and *Store_Receipt*. The former is invoked by S whenever he wants to forward a certified email message. The latter is invoked by the TTP at the moment the receiver accepts and reads the message. The receipt is verified and stored and made available to S.

- **Receiver's Webmail Server** (WMS_R): The WMS_R exposes the *Store_Message* service which is called by the WMS_S in order to store a delivered email message. Receiver server invokes also a service on TTP to obtain data to generate the decryption key. Furthermore, this server provides to store cipher and plain mail.

- **TTP Server:** The TTP exposes the $Key\_Request$ service which is invoked by the WMS_R during the reading of a certified email message in order to retrieve the decryption key associated with the messageǔ

Both sender's and receiver's Webmail servers allow users to access one's mailbox through web pages using a standard Internet browser. In addition to

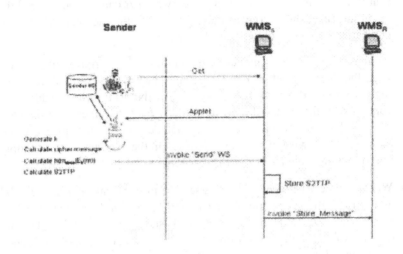

the standard functions of an e-mail client, such servers offer the functionalities of composing and receiving certified email messages, in a (as much as possible) transparent way for the users, which are requested to provide the data necessary to execute the phases of the protocol. We assume that the communication channel among the participants are secured using standard techniques, like SSL. To this purpose it is important that both S and R know the public key of the TTP and are able to establish a secured connection with their respective Webmail servers by authenticating themselves (e.g., via login and password). The communication among the Webmail servers and the TTP should be secured using strong authentication mechanisms (via certificate exchange).

Let us show in more detail the interactions occurring during the sending and the reading of the mail. As shown in figure 2, in order to send a certified email message, the sender invokes the $Send$ service provided by WMS_S. To this purposes he constructs a SOAP message which encloses all the data needed to follow the protocol above described. On the server side, the message is processed such that the data needed to construct the SOAP message containing the request to the WMS_R $Store\_Message$ service are retrieved. The WMS_R stores the message such that R is displayed the notification of a received certified email message.

If R is interested in reading the certified email message, a SOAP message containing the $Key\_Request$ service invocation is constructed and forwarded to the TTPserver. Such request contains the $S2TTP$ which the TTP can de-

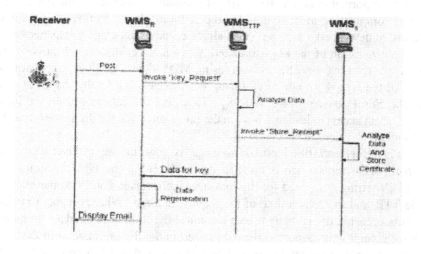

Figure 3.   Reading Email

crypt in order to recovery the key associated with the message together with the hash of the subject of the email and the encrypted message. According to the protocol, on a successful checking of the validity of the received data, the TTP invokes the $Store\_Receipt$ service on the WMS_S, which enables the sender to get a valid receipt, and constructs the response message for the WMS_R, which enables R to decrypt and read the mail message.

5.   Implementation

The implementation and the deployment of Web services applications involve several critical aspects which must be taken into account in order to satisfy the security requirements. We developed a prototype implementation of the proposed certified email system using Java (version 1.4.2) as development language. Java offers also a comprehensive set of cryptographic tools and libraries which have been used in order to execute the operations needed to execute the protocol. Some of the needed cryptographic functions have been implemented using the BouncyCastle Cryptographic Service Provider.

As application server we used Tomcat (version 4.1), usually referred as the official implementation for the Java Servlet and JavaServer Pages technologies. The SOAP engine is provided by Apache Axis (version 1.1) which offers a framework for constructing SOAP processors, a server which plugs into servlet engines (such as Tomcat), extensive support for the Web Service Description Language (WSDL), together with a set of other useful tools for the development phase.

It is important to notice that during the sending of a certified email message, some computation must be done on the client machine. To this aim an applet has been developed which performs all the cryptographic operations necessary to the generation of the key associated with a new certified email message, its encryption (using 3-DES), its hash (using MD5 digest function), the computation of the signed string S2TTP (using RSA-SHA1) and finally the invocation of the *Send* service on the WMS_S. To access the data stored on the local disk, some access-rules contained in the java-policy file for the sender must be modified.

Whenever a certified email message is sent to the receiver, i.e., the *Store_Message* service is invoked on the WMS_R, the WMS_S stores the $S2TTP$ string computed for the message, the receiver's address, the URL of the TTP, and the arrival time of the request in a file. Whenever the TTP forwards a receipt, the WMS_S is able to control the validity of the data contained in the receipt with respect to the data stored in the file associate with the message. If the data match, the signed receipt is stored and can be used by S in case of dispute.

On the receiver's side, if R decides to read a certified email message, at the end of the interaction between the WMS_R and the TTP, the notification is substituted with the decrypted copy of the message.

6.   Discussion

As discussed in [AHGP02], some of the security properties presented in section 2 are satisfied by the protocol and the service implementation we proposed. In particular, the implementation provides confidentiality and integrity of the mail messages. Indeed, confidentiality with respect to external users and the TTP is guaranteed by the assumption that all the communication channel are secured, and the message is encrypted with the session key k. Cleartext message is not known to the WMS_S and the TTP, but only to the WMS_R after the completion of the protocol (since the decrypted message is stored in the mailbox of R like ordinary email messages). To increase the confidentiality of the exchange, and avoid that the WMS_R knows the decrypted message, it is possible to execute the decryption operation directly on R's local machine.

Fairness and non repudiation of receipt properties are also satisfied. If both the sender and the receiver behave as expected and messages are delivered, at the end of the protocol each party gets the desired information. The protocol implementation relies on the TTP server in order to ensure that after a message exchange, R is able to read the email if and only if S receives the corresponding return receipt. Indeed, at the end of the protocol execution, S can show in case of dispute the message $S2TTP$ signed by the TTP, which constitutes a non repudiable certification of the reception of the message by R.

7.   Conclusions

The emerging Web services standards provides a new technology supporting the release of Web based applications. Such new paradigm of computing allows the development of distributed applications, realized through loosely coupled collaborating services which implement business processes and are available through the Internet to end users [CCS03].

In this work we experimented the design and the implementation of a certified email service. Usually other approaches [AHGP02] require the users to install some additional software, such as a plug-in tailored to a particular email client or Internet browser. Such an approach limits the number of target users, since they are usually reluctant to modify or install software on the local machines. Other approaches rely on the development of a mail proxy, which filters incoming and outcoming messages, executing transparently the certified email protocol. But also in this case users should trust and use an additional piece of software. The proposed Web system does not require any additional software apart from a Java enabled browser (and some modification to the Java local policy file). We plan to extend the approach to the implementation of other email protocols, satisfying a larger number of security properties achieved through the combination of simpler available services.

References

[ASW97] Asokan, N., Schunter, M., and Waidner, M., 1997, Optimistic Protocols for Fair Exchange, In *ACM Conference on Computer and Communications Security*, pp. 7–17.

[ASW98] Asokan, N., Shoup, V., and Waidner, M., 1998, Asynchronous Protocols for Optimistic Fair Exchange, In *Proceedings of the IEEE Symposium on Research in Security and Privacy*, pp 86–99.

[BT94] Bahreman, A., and Tygar, J. D., 1994. Certified Electronic Mail. In Dan Nesset (General Chair) and Robj Shirey (Program Chair), editors, *Proceedings of the Symposium on Network and Distributed Systems Security*, California, Internet Society, pp 3–19.

[Blu83] Blum, M., 1983, How to Exchange (Secret) Keys, In *STOC*, pp 440–447.

[Bro03] Brose, G., 2003, A Gateway to Web Services Security – Securing SOAP with Proxies, In *Proceedings of International Conference on Web Services-Europe 2003 (ICWS-Europe 2003)*, Lecture Notes in Computer Science, vol. 2853, pp. 101-108.

[CCS03] Chen, M., Chen, A. N. K., and Shao. B., 2003, The Implications and Impact of Web Services to Electronic Commerce Research and Practices, *Journal Electronic Commerce Research*, Vol. 4, N. 4.

[CGKL+02] Curbera, F., Goland, Y., Klein, J., Leymann, F., Roller, D., Thatte, D., and Weerawarana, S., 2002, Business Process Execution Language for Web Services (BPEL4WS 1.0).

[DGLW96] Deng, R. H., Gong, L., Lazar, A. A., and Wang, W., 1996, Practical protocols for Certified Electronic Mail, *Journal of Network and System Management*, 4(3).

[AHGP02] Abadi, M., Horne, B., Glew, N., and Pinkas, B., 2002, Certified Email with a Light On-Line Trusted Third Party: Design and Implementation, In *Proceedings of eleventh International World Wide Web Conference*, ACM Press, New York.

[EGL85] Even, S., Goldreich, O., and Lempel, A., 1985, A Randomized Protocol for Signing Contracts, *Communications of the ACM*, 28(6).

[Ley01] Leymann, F., 2001, Web Services Flow Language (WSFL 1.0) IBM Software Group.

[RS98] Riordan, J., and Schneier, B., 1998, A certified E-mail protocol with No Trusted Third Party, In *Proceedings of the 13th Annual Computer Security Applications Conference.*

[Tha01] Thatte, S., 2001, XLANG: Web Services for Business Process Design, Microsoft Corporation.

[GZ96] Gollmann, D., and Zhou, J., 1996, A Fair Non-Repudiation Protocol, In *Proceedings of the IEEE Symposium on Research in Security and Privacy*, CA. IEEE Computer Society Press, Oakland, pp 55–61.

TRUTHFUL MECHANISMS FOR BUILDING TRUST IN E-COMMERCE

Giovanna Melideo[1] and Guido Proietti[1,2]

[1]*Dipartimento di Informatica, Università di L'Aquila, Via Vetoio, 67010 L'Aquila, Italy*

[2]*Istituto di Analisi dei Sistemi ed Informatica, CNR, Viale Manzoni 30, 00185 Roma, Italy*
{melideo,proietti}@di.univaq.it

Abstract

A fundamental issue for a real uptake of commercial transactions over the web regards *trust* among the transacting entities, frequently unknown to each other. One solution to increase confidence in transactions is to use a network of TSPs (Trust Service Providers), called a *trust web*, which are third parties known and trusted by both entities, and an algorithm that establishes a trust path before carrying-out any e-commerce transaction.

In this paper we study the problem of building trust paths linking an entity initiating a transaction to a set of final merchants in a trust web from a "mechanism design" point of view. Namely, we consider TSPs as *strategic agents* which respond to incentives and may deviate from the protocol for a tangible gain. A *truthful* mechanism should define both the protocol and a suitable payment rule such that each agent maximizes her own utility when not deviating from the protocol, regardless of what other agents do.

We first address the problem from a "protocol design" perspective and, assuming that TSPs are *honest/obedient*, we propose a distributed search algorithm based on a *probabilistic* trust degree model [Mau96, DIM02] which generalizes that based only on boolean trust relationships proposed in [Ati02], and reduces the search space complexity by pruning the alternatives that do not satisfy (besides cost constraints) trust degree constraints (e.g., the "transitive" degree of trust accumulated along the path has to be greater than a given threshold value).

Then, when considering TSPs as *strategic agents*, we use this algorithm as a substrate to define truthful mechanisms for building suitable trust paths. Indeed, the main scope of this paper is to provide an answer to the following fundamental problem: does a payment function exist for the described problem such that the the resulting mechanism is truthful? By applying recent results appeared in [MPPW+04] we provide both positive and negative answers, depending on which constraint we add/drop and on which parameters are considered as a private information of agents.

Keywords: Algorithmic Mechanism Design, Algorithms for the Internet, Game Theory, Trust, e-Commerce, Security Services, Public Key Certification

1. Introduction

Internet services are increasingly being used in daily life for e-commerce, web-access to information and inter-personal interactions via e-mail, but there is still major concern about the trustworthiness of these e-services.

Trust is a fundamental component in every business transaction. Customers must trust that merchants will provide the services that they advertise, will not disclose nor misuse private customer information such as its credit card number. Trust in the supplier's competence and honesty will influence the customer's decision as to which supplier to use. Merchants must trust that the buyer is able to pay for goods or services. Hence, for e-commerce to achieve the same levels of acceptance as traditional commerce, trust management has to be an intrinsic part of e-commerce.

More and more often, to increase confidence in commercial transactions over the Web, where the transacting parts are frequently unknown to each other, the design of new protocol is based on the enlistment of a third party, referred to as a *trust service provider* (TSP), acting as a trusted intermediary which assumes responsibility for a smooth transaction. TSPs are known and trusted by both customer and merchant.

Following [Ati02, CAR00, HFH99, DIM02], from a graph-theoretical point of view such a network of trusted intermediaries (referred to as *trust web*) can be modelled as a *trust graph*, where vertices denote the TSPs and edges reflet trust relationships between TSPs. Each TSP only knows its immediate trusted neighbors rather than each TSP in the global trust web.

A typical e-commerce transaction follows three steps: (i) locating business entities, (ii) establishing a trust path (i.e., a chain of TSPs linking the customer with the final merchant), and (iii) executing the transaction along the best-suited trust path. Successful e-commerce systems depend heavily on the second step. A trust relationship is established by an initiating entity that wishes to build a relationship with another selected entity by some means, such a private relationship, positive past experience or simply by reputation. This form of Internet-base mediation can be iteratively extended when the customer does not have a direct trust link with the final merchant [Ati02, DIM02].

To the best of our knowledge, the problem of building trust paths has been only studied from a "protocol design" perspective, by assuming that all the TSPs are *honest/obedient*, that is that they follows the protocol. In [Ati02, SM97] a distributed search algorithm has been proposed aimed at identifying a trust path linking an initiating entity e (the customer) with a set F of final merchants across a chain of TSPs such that each TSP trusts its immediate neighbors. The algorithm requires the cooperation of multiple TSPs to find trust paths. The trust web's connectivity might be high, i.e., each TSP vertex might be linked to several other TSPs, increasing the complexity of the search process. The search space complexity can be then reduced by pruning the alternatives that do not satisfy suitable constraints, such as cost constraints (e.g., the transmission cost accumulated along the path has not to exceed a given threshold cost β).

However, the complex economic context can have a deep influence on the design process, in that if a protocol is demonstrated to have a good performance, this does not necessarily mean that it will be successful. For this protocol to be "fit", the design must be paved with *incentives* that will motivate all the participant TSPs to adopt it. Indeed, all the TSPs are actually *strategic agents* which respond to incentives and will deviate from the protocol only for a tangible gain. Mechanism design asks how one can design systems so that agents' selfish behavior results in the desired system-wide goals. That is, a mechanism should define both (i) the protocol and (ii) a suitable *payment rule* such that each agent maximizes her own utility without deviating, regardless of what other agents do. A mechanism which guarantees this property for every agent is called a *truthful mechanism*.

As regards the protocol, the model proposed in [Ati02, SM97] is based only on boolean relationships, i.e., any two entities can share either a complete trust or a complete distrust relationship. A *probabilistic trust model* based on values on a continuous scale in $[0, 1]$ has been considered in [Mau96, DIM02] for determining the most trusted path between two entities in authentication infrastructures based on public key certificates (PKI). *Authentication* is the verification of an identity of an entity, which may be performed by means of a trusted authentication service or using *certificates*[1] . There is then an issue of the degree of trust in the entity which released the certificate. Basing on this model, the degree $d_{i,j}$ of entity i's trust in entity j has been interpreted as the probability that the certificates issued by j are correct. In this paper we will adopt the probabilistic trust model and we interpret, more in general, the degree of trust in a TSP as the probability that she is capable of performing the expected functions, or the service she is meant to provide correctly and within reasonable timescales. We will incorporate such a probabilistic model in the distributed search algorithm described in [Ati02] for determining the best-suited trust paths by also pruning alternatives that does not satisfy (besides cost constraints) trust degree constraints: the "transitive" degree of trust accumulated along the path has to be greater than a given threshold value α.

More precisely, we propose an extended search algorithm (see Section 5) which allows to solve the two problems defined as follows: given a initiating entity (costumer) e, a set of final entities (merchants) F, a threshold degree of trust $\alpha \in (0, 1]$, and a threshold communication cost $\beta \in I\!\!R^+$, establish a set of trust paths linking e to the final entities in such a way to satisfy both cost and trust degree constraints and then find either (i) the lowest cost trust paths reaching located merchants, or (ii) the most trusted paths reaching located merchants. We will refer to these two problems as the *min-cost-TP[e, F, α, β]* and the *max-trust-TP[e, F, α, β]* problem, respectively.

Then, we use the proposed algorithmic approach as a substrate to address the problem also from a *mechanism design* point of view. The main scope of this paper is to provide an answer to the following fundamental problem: does a payment function exist for the described problems such that the the resulting mechanism is truthful? By applying recent results appeared in [MPPW⁺04] and reviewed in Section 2, we provide both positive and negative answers, depending on which constraint we add/drop and on which parameters are considered as a private information of agents. In particular, we provide two distinct truthful mechanisms, called the *marginal transaction cost mechanism* and the *marginal trust mechanism*, as the solutions of two special cases of the defined problems.

2. Algorithmic mechanism design

In this section we review the basics of algorithmic mechanism design. For a more extensive discussion of applications of game theoretic tools and microeconomics to the Internet we refer the reader to [AT01, FPS01, FS02, NR99, NR00, Pap01]. In designing network protocols computer scientists typically assume that the entities involved in the computation are either *honest/obedient* (i.e., they follow the protocol) or *adversarial* (i.e., they "play against"). In contrast, game theorists study what happens when independent entities (also called *agents* or *players*) are *strategic* and respond to *incentives* (e.g., a payment received to compensate the costs). Mechanism design asks how one can design systems so that agents selfish behavior results in the desired system-wide goals.

In the standard model for the design and analysis of scenarios involving entities which act according to their own self-interest, there are n agents $\{1, \dots, n\}$ each one holding some private information t_i, called its *type* and belonging to a type space T_i.

A *mechanism design problem* is characterized by an *output specification* $o(\cdot)$ mapping each type vector $t = (t_1, \dots, t_n)$ to a set of feasible outputs Φ. Each agent is assumed to incur some intrinsic benefit or loss $v_i(x, t_i)$, called its *valuation*, which depends on the considered output x. A mechanism defines for each vector $r = (r_1, \dots, r_n)$ (called the *input vector*), with $r_i \in T_i$, (i) an output $x = o(r)$ and (ii) a *payment vector* $p(r) = (p_1(r), \dots, p_n(r))$. Each agent i gives $r_i \in T_i$ as input (i.e., agent i plays r_i) in order to maximize her own *utility* $u_i(o(r), t_i, p_i(r))$, expressible as a function of the output $x = o(r)$, the valuation $v_i(x, t_i)$ and the payment $p_i(r)$. Therefore, one should design both (i) an algorithm $\mathcal{A}$ which computes $o(\cdot)$ and (ii) a suitable payment rule

$p(\cdot)$ such that each agent maximizes her utility by "playing" the type $r_i = t_i$ regardless of what other agents do. In other words, if r^{-i} denotes a vector of inputs given by all agents except agent i, the relation

$$u_i(o(r^{-i}, t_i), t_i, p_i(r^{-i}, t_i)) \geq u_i(o(r^{-i}, r_i), t_i, p_i(r^{-i}, r_i)) \qquad (1)$$

must hold for all i and all possible values of t_i, r^{-i} and r_i.

The pair $(\mathcal{A}, p)$ that allows to guarantee Property (1) for every agent is called a *truthful mechanism* with dominant strategies. Hence, a mechanism wants each agent to report her type truthfully, and it is allowed to pay agents in order to provide incentives for them to do so.

A large body of the existing literature focuses on the class of problems in which the utilities are *quasi-linear*, that is, agent i's utility factors into $u_i(o(r), t_i, p_i(r)) = v_i(o(r), t_i) + p_i(r)$. For such problems, the celebrated Vickrey-Clarke-Groves (VCG) mechanisms [Cla71, Gro73, Vic61] guarantee the truthfulness under the hypothesis that the algorithm maximizes the objective function $\mu(x, r) = \sum_i v_i(x, r_i)$. VCG mechanisms have been successfully applied to a multitude of optimization problems involving selfish agents with applications to networking [FPS01, NR00] and e-commerce [Cra97]. All these works assume that the problem is *utilitarian*, that is, the utility functions are quasi-linear and the objective function can be written as the sum above.

Recently, a class of optimization problems has been defined in [MPPW⁺04], termed *consistent problems*, which are mechanism design problems such that:

(a) the set of feasible solutions Φ does not depend on agents' types;

(b) the *consistent objective function* is expressible as $\mu(x, r) = \bigoplus_i v_i(x, r_i)$ for a suitable operator $\oplus$ which enjoys the following properties: associativity, commutativity and monotonicity in its arguments;

(c) the utility function is expressible as $u_i(o(r), t_i, p_i(r)) = v_i(o(r), t_i) \oplus p_i(r)$.

The authors proved that consistent problems admit truthful mechanisms, called *VCG-consistent* (VCGc) mechanisms and defined as a natural extension of VCG mechanisms. If the operator also enjoys the following properties: identity element, inverse and strict monotonicity, the VCGc mechanisms are the only truthful mechanisms for the problem. The characterization of VCGc mechanisms states that the payment functions $p_i(\cdot)$ provided from a truthful mechanism for a consistent problem can be expressed as $p_i(r) = \bigoplus_{j \neq i} v_j(o(r), r_j) \oplus h_i(r^{-i})$, where $h_i(\cdot)$ is a function of r^{-i}. Interestingly, it has been also identified a subclass of non-consistent problems in which the set of feasible solutions Φ depends on agents' types which does not admit truthful mechanism.

3.   The model

We consider a graph-theoretic model for the *trust web* referred to here as the *trust graph* and composed of:

- a set $V = \{1, \ldots, n\}$ of weighted vertices (the agents) denoting each a TSP whose weight $c_i \in I\!R^+$ represents the cost TSP i incurs for executing each transaction;
- a set E of weighted directed edges $\langle i, j \rangle \in V \times V$, which reflect trust relationships, whose weight $d_{i,j} \in (0, 1]$ denotes the degree of trust of i in j, according to the probabilistic model proposed in [Mau96, DIM02].

From now on we will adopt the following notations. Let $\mathcal{E}$ be any set of potential transacting entities (e.g., consumers and merchants) such that $V \cap \mathcal{E} = \emptyset$. We will refer to e as the entity in $\mathcal{E}$ initiating a request for carrying out an e-commerce transaction (said a consumer) to acquire commodities from a set of final entities f (merchants). For any TSP $i \in V$, $\mathcal{E}[i] \subseteq \mathcal{E}$ denotes all the entities that know and trust TSP i directly, and, for any $x \in \mathcal{E}$, $V[x] \subseteq V$ is the subset of TSPs known and trusted by x, i.e., $V[x] = \{i \in V \mid x \in \mathcal{E}(i)\}$. Finally, for each TSP i, we will denote by $N(i)$ the set of neighbors of i in the trust graph.

DEFINITION 1 *A trust path $\pi(e, f)$ linking e to f is a chain of TSPs $\langle i_1, \ldots, i_k \rangle$ such that $e \in \mathcal{E}(i_1)$, $f \in \mathcal{E}(i_k)$, and for each $j = 2, \ldots, k$, it holds $i_j \in N(i_{j-1})$.*

DEFINITION 2 *The transaction cost of a trust path π, denoted by $cost(\pi)$, is the overall cost incurred by each TSP i on the path, i.e., $cost(\pi) = \sum_{i \in \pi} c_i$.*

DEFINITION 3 *The degree of a trust path $\pi = \langle i_1, \ldots, i_k \rangle$, denoted by $d(\pi)$, is the "transitive" degree of trust induced by π, i.e., $d(\pi) = \prod_{j=1}^{k-1} d_{i_j, i_{j+1}}$.*

Let $\Pi(e, f)$ be the set of all the different trust paths in the trust graph linking e to f.

DEFINITION 4 (THE LOWEST-COST TRUST PATH) *The lowest-cost trust path $\pi_{LC}(e, f)$ linking e to f is the trust path in $\Pi(e, f)$ of minimum transaction cost.*

DEFINITION 5 (THE MOST-TRUSTED PATH) *The most-trusted path $\pi_{MT}(e, f)$ linking e to f is the trust path in $\Pi(e, f)$ of maximum transitive trust degree.*

4.   The problems

A typical e-commerce transaction for acquiring commodities from a set of merchants F (final entities or targets) consists of the following steps:

- Locating a set $R \subseteq F$ of reachable final merchants.
  Let ρ denote the characteristic function associated with R, i.e., $\rho(f) = 1$ for every $f \in R$, $\rho(f) = 0$ otherwise.
- Constructing a set of trust paths $\Pi(e, R, \alpha, \beta)$ linking e to finals in R, where α e β are two parameters whose meaning will be clear later.
  We denote by $\Pi(e, f, \alpha, \beta) \subseteq \Pi(e, R, \alpha, \beta)$ the subset of trust paths linking e to f.
- For any final $f \in R$, executing the transaction along either (i) a lowest-cost trust path $\pi_{LC}(e, f) \in \Pi(e, f, \alpha, \beta)$ (see Def. 6), or (ii) a most-trusted path $\pi_{MT}(e, f) \in \Pi(e, f, \alpha, \beta)$ (see Def. 7).
  Let χ_{LC} and χ_{MT} be the characteristic functions for the lowest-cost trust path and the most-trusted path, respectively, i.e., $\chi_{LC}(i, e, f) = 1$ if $i \in V$ is on the path $\pi_{LC}(e, f)$ and $\chi_{LC}(i, e, f) = 0$ otherwise, and $\chi_{MT}(i, e, f) = 1$ if $i \in V$ is on the path $\pi_{MT}(e, f)$ and $\chi_{MT}(i, e, f) = 0$ otherwise.

Minimizing for every $f \in R$ the cost of the trust path linking e to f is equivalent to minimizing the overall transaction cost. Hence:

DEFINITION 6 *For every feasible output* $x = (\rho, \chi_{LC})$, *the* min-cost-TP[e, F, \alpha, \beta] problem *aims to minimize the following objective function:*

$$\mu_{LC}(x, e, F, \alpha, \beta) = \sum_{f \in F} \rho(f) \sum_{i \in V} c_i \cdot \chi_{LC}(i, e, f). \qquad (2)$$

Equivalently:

DEFINITION 7 *For every feasible output* $x = (\rho, \chi_{MT})$, *the* max-trust-TP[e, F, \alpha, \beta] problem *aims to maximize the following objective function:*

$$\mu_{MT}(x, e, F, \alpha, \beta) = \prod_{f \in F} \rho(f) \prod_{i \in V} \chi_{MT}(i, e, f) \left(\sum_{\langle i,j \rangle \in E} \chi_{MT}(j, e, f) \cdot d_{i,j} \right).$$
$$(3)$$

5. The trust paths building algorithm

In this section we describe a search algorithm $\mathcal{A}$ which solves the just introduced problems. In order to identifying the best-suited trust paths, as each TSP within the trust web knows only its immediate trusted neighbors (each $i \in V$ only knows adjacent vertices $N(i)$ within the trust graph) rather than each TSP within the global trust web, the algorithm $\mathcal{A}$ requires the cooperation of multiple TPSs.

When a customer e initiates the search process, it relies the final merchants F automatically to the nearest trusted TSPs $V[e]$ in hopes of finding the finals. If these TSPs do not have direct trust relationships with the finals, they *forward* the customer's request to the adjacent TSPs to identify finals deeper within the trust graph. Therefore, the search of finals generates *forward messages*. A TSP stops the search when there are no connections or all its connections lead to already explored TSPs[2], or when all the connections lead to "unreliable" ot "too expensive" trust paths. Indeed, the search space complexity and the number of messages exchanged between TSPs is reduced by pruning the alternatives π that does not satisfy these constraints:

- *Trust constraint*: the trust degree accumulated along the path is greater than a threshold trust degree $\alpha \in [0, 1]$, i.e., $d(\pi) = \prod_{\langle i,j \rangle \in \pi} \geq \alpha$;
- *Cost constraint*: the transaction cost accumulated along the path is less than a threshold cost $\beta \in \mathbb{R}^+$, i.e, $cost(\pi) = \sum_{i \in \pi} c_i \leq \beta$.

When finals have been located, *backward messages* trace the path of the forward messages back to e. If e does not receive a backward message after a certain time, it assumes that no path was found.

The structure of a *forward message* $m = \{e, F, \alpha, \beta, \pi_r, d(\pi_r), cost(\pi_r)\}$ specifies (among the others):

- the costumer e and the list of final merchants F to be located;
- a threshold trust degree $\alpha \in [0, 1]$ and a threshold transaction cost $\beta \in \mathbb{R}^+$;
- a *return path* π_r containing a sequence initially empty of 4-tuples

$$\langle (i_1, F_{i_1}, d_{e,i_1} = 1, c_{i_1}), \ldots, (i_h, F_{i_h}, d_{i_{h-1}, i_h}, c_{i_h}) \rangle$$

where $\langle i_1, \ldots i_h \rangle$ is the identified path $\pi(e, i_h)$ and, for any TSP i_j on it, F_{i_j} is the set of identified targets that i_j knows and trusts directly;
- the trust degree $d(\pi_r) = d(\pi(e, i_h))$ accumulated along the path $\pi(e, i_h)$;
- the transaction cost $cost(\pi_r) = cost(\pi(e, i_h))$ accumulated along the path $\pi(e, i_h)$.

For a message $m = \{e, F, \alpha, \beta, \pi_r, d(\pi_r), cost(\pi_r)\}$ identifying a trust path $\pi(e, i)$, we say that a TSP j is *appended* to m if:

- the 4-tuple $(j, F \cap \mathcal{E}[j], d_{i,j}, c_j)$ is added to the return path π_r;
- F is updated to the set of TSPs left to locate, i.e., $F = F \setminus \mathcal{E}[j]$;
- the trust degree is updated to $d(\pi_r) \cdot d_{i,j}$;
- the transaction cost is updated to $cost(\pi_r) + c_j$.

The resulting message is denoted by $append(m, i, j)$.

The algorithm works as follows (due to lack of space details concerning the backward phase will be omitted):

- Initially, if customer e neither knows nor trusts finals in F, it prepares the initial forward message $m = \{e, F, \alpha, \beta, \pi_r = \emptyset, d(\pi_r) = 1, cost(\pi_r) = 0\}$ and sends it in parallel to all trusted TSPs $j \in V[e]$. Without loss of generality, we assume that consumers/merchants completely trust TSPs they know directly (i.e., $d_{e,j} = 1, \forall j \in V[e]$).

- On receiving a message $m = \{e. F. \alpha, \beta, \pi_r, d(\pi_r), cost(\pi_r)\}$ from i a TSP j executes the following steps:

  - let $N(j)' = \{k \in N(j) \mid k$ is unvisited $\wedge \; d(\pi_r) \cdot d_{j,k} \geq \alpha\}$;
  - if $cost(\pi_r) + c_j > \beta \vee N(j)' = \emptyset$ (this is a dead end) then

    if $F \cap \mathcal{E}[j] = \emptyset$ then j sends m backward to i
    else j sends $append(m, i, j)$ backward to i;

    else j forwards $append(m, i, j)$ to each $k \in N(j)'$.

6. The mechanism design trust paths building problems

The algorithm just described assumes that that all the reached TSPs are *honest/obedient*, that is that they follows the protocol when reporting their transaction costs and the degrees of trust in the neighbors, which are both a private information of TSPs (their types). However, all the TSPs are actually *strategic agents* which respond to incentives and may deviate from the protocol for a tangible gain. Hence, for this algorithm to be "fit", the design must be paved with suitable *payments* that will motivate all the participant TSPs to adopt it.

In this section we aim to answer the following central question about the study of which goals are achievable via truthful mechanisms, that is "does a payment function $p(\cdot)$ exist such that the resulting mechanism is truthful?"

Towards this aim, we need to define the trust path building problem as a consistent problem which we know to admit truthful mechanisms. It is worthy to notice that we provide a payment specified by $p_i(\cdot)$ to a TSP i if and only if i is on one of the established trust paths linking the consumer e to some merchant in F.

Since e-commerce transactions are executed along either the most trusted paths or the lowest cost trust paths, the definition of *consistent problem* (requiring that the set of feasible solutions does not depend on agents' types) points to only two distinct mechanisms, the *marginal transaction cost mechanism* and the *marginal trust mechanism* as the two solutions of the two mechanism design problems defined in Sections 6 and 6.

The min-cost-TP[e, F, α] problem

Given the set $V = \{1, \ldots, n\}$ of agents (TSPs within the trust web), formulating the *min-cost-TP[e, F, α, β]* problem as a mechanism design consistent problem basically requires (i) to define agent's types and prove that the set of feasible solutions Φ is independent of them; (ii) to define the valuation functions $v_i(\cdot)$ and show that the objective function is of the form $\bigoplus_{i=1}^{n} v_i(\cdot)$, where $\uplus$ is a suitable operator which enjoys the following properties: associativity, commutativity and monotonicity in its arguments; (iv) to express in a "consistent" way the utility functions as $u_i(\cdot) = p_i(\cdot) \oplus v_i(\cdot)$ for appropriate payment functions $p_i(\cdot)$.

The scenario described until now considers each TSP i as a strategic agent which knows both the transaction cost c_i and the degrees of trust. However, by following this model the set of feasible solutions would completely depend on agents' types. These dependencies would affect the existence of truthful mechanisms for the problem [MPPW+04]. Hence, the only way to structure the problem as a consistent problem is to make feasible solutions $x = (\rho, \chi_{LC})$ independent of transaction costs by assuming a modified scenario where:

- degrees of trust are publicly known and agent i's type is the transaction cost $t_i = c_i$, for each $i \in V$;
- the search space is not reduced by applying cost constraints.

We denote such a subproblem by *min-cost-TP*$[e, F, \alpha]$.

It is immediate to verify that the function (2) is a *utilitarian* objective function (i.e., a consistent objective function whose operator is the sum) by defining the valuation functions as follows: for any reported vector of costs r and for any feasible output $x = (\rho, \chi_{LC})$, i.e., a set of located finals $R \subseteq F$ and a set of trust paths each linking e to a final entity $f \in R$, we have

$$v_i(x, r_i) = \sum_{f \in F} \rho(f) \cdot r_i \cdot \chi_{LC}(i, e, f). \qquad (4)$$

THEOREM 8 *When the distributed algorithm $\mathcal{A}$ outputs a solution $x^* = (\rho, \chi_{LC})$ inducing on the trust graph G a biconnected subgraph and picks lowest cost paths linking e to the reachable finals, then there is a unique truthful mechanism $(\mathcal{A}, p)$ for the* min-cost-TP$[e, F, \alpha]$ *problem that gives no payment to TSPs not involved in transactions.*

Proof. For any reported vector of costs r and for any feasible solution x, let us denote by $\mu_{LC}(x, r) = \sum_{i=1}^{n} v_i(x, r_i)$ the overall transition cost of the solution. Moreover, let $\mu_{LC}^{-i}(x, r) = \sum_{j \neq i}^{n} v_j(x, r_j)$. For utilitarian problems, VCG mechanisms [Cla71, Gro73, Vic61] guarantee the truthfulness of the mechanism $(\mathcal{A}, p)$ when the payments to the involved TSPs i are of the form: $p_i(r) = \mu_{LC}(\mathcal{A}(r^{-i}, r_i = \infty), r) - \mu_{LC}^{-i}(\mathcal{A}(r), r)$. $\square$

The max-trust-TP$[e, F, \beta]$ problem

Similarly to the *min-cost-TP*$[e, F, \alpha, \beta]$ problem, in order to formulate the *max-trust-TP*$[e, F, \alpha, \beta]$ problem as a mechanism design consistent problem we need to make feasible outputs $x = (\rho, \chi_{MT})$ independent of degrees of trust by assuming a modified scenario where:

- costs are publicly known and agent i's type is the vector t_i of degrees of trust $t_i^j = d_{i,j}$, for each $j \in N(i)$;
- the search space is not reduced by applying trust constraints.

We denote such a subproblem by *max-trust-TP*$[e, F, \beta]$.

In order to prove that the function (3) is a consistent objective function whose operator is the standard product, we define the valuation functions as follows. For any reported degrees of trust r and for any feasible output $x = (\rho, \chi_{MT})$:

$$v_i(x, r_i) = \prod_{f \in F} v_i^f(x, r_i) \quad \text{such that}$$

$$v_i^f(x, r_i) = \begin{cases} \sum_{\langle i,j \rangle \in E} r_i^j \cdot \chi_{MT}(j, e, f) & \text{if } \rho(f) + \chi_{MT}(i, e, f) = 2; \\ 1 & \text{otherwise.} \end{cases}$$

THEOREM 9 *When the distributed algorithm $\mathcal{A}$ outputs a solution $x^* = (\rho, \chi_{MT})$ inducing on the trust graph G a biconnected subgraph and picks most trusted paths linking e to the reachable finals, then there exists a truthful mechanism $(\mathcal{A}, p)$ for the* max-trust-TP$[e, F, \beta]$ *problem that gives no payment to TSPs not involved in transactions.*

Proof. For any feasible solution x and for any reported vector of degrees of trust r, let $\mu_{MT}(x, r) = \prod_{i=1}^{n} v_i(x, r_i)$ be the overall trust degree of the solution and let $\mu_{MT}^{-i}(x, r) = \prod_{j \neq i}^{n} v_j(x, r_j)$. For consistent problems, the VCGc mechanisms recently introduced in [MPPW+04] guarantee the truthfulness of the mechanism $(\mathcal{A}, p)$ when the payments to the involved TSPs i are of the form:

$$p_i(r) = \frac{\mu_{MT}^{-i}(\mathcal{A}(r), r)}{\mu_{MT}(\mathcal{A}(r^{-i}, r_i = 0), r)}.$$

$\square$

Acknowledgments

This work has been developed within the activities of the Research Project GRID.IT, funded by the Italian Ministry of Education, University and Research, and whose support is gratefully acknowledged. The authors would also like to thank Enrico Nardelli for useful discussions on the topic presented here.

Notes

1. A certificate is a digitally signed statement by which a trusted third party, referred to as a *Certification Authority* (CA), asserts that a public key is bound to an entity. The term PKI is used to refer to an infrastructure for distributing public keys, where the authenticity of public keys is certified by the CAs.

2. To avoid a TSP receive and process the same request twice we suppose that (i) each request includes a unique session ID and time-stamps, (ii) all received requests are backlogged and (iii) duplicated requests are discarded.

References

[AT01]   A. Archer and E. Tardos. Truthful mechanisms for one-parameter agents. In *Proc. of the 42nd Annual Symposium on Foundations of Computer Science (FOCS'01)*, 482–491, 2001.

[Ati02]   Y. Atif. Building Trust in E-Commerce. *IEEE Internet Computing*, 6(1):18–24, 2002.

[CAR00]   G. Caronni. Walking the web of trust. In *Proc. of 9th Workshop on Enabling Technologies (WETICE 2000)*, IEEE Computer Society Press, 153–158, 2000.

[Cla71]   E. Clarke. Multipart pricing of public goods. *Public Choice*, 8:17–33, 1971.

[Col90]   J. Coleman. *Foundations of Social Theory*. Harvard University Press, 1990.

[Cra97]   P. Cramton. The FCC spectrum auction: an early assessment. *Journal of Economics and Management Strategy*, 6:431–495, 1997.

[FPS01]   J. Feigenbaum, C.H. Papadimitriou, and S. Shenker. Sharing the cost of multicast transmissions. *Journal of Computer and System Sciences*, 63(1):21–41, 2001.

[FS02]   J. Feigenbaum and S. Shenker. Distributed algorithmic mechanism design: Recent results and future directions. In *Proc. of the 6th International Workshop on Discrete Algorithms and Methods for Mobile Computing and Communications*, ACM Press, 1–13, 2002.

[GL77]   J. Green and J.J. Laffont. Characterization of satisfactory mechanisms for the revelation of preferences for public goods. *Econometrica*, 45(2):727–738, 1977.

[Gro73]   T. Groves. Incentives in teams. *Econometrica*, 41(4):617–631, 1973.

[HFH99]   B.A. Hubermann, M. Franklin, and T. Hogg. Enhancing privacy and trust in electronic communities. In *Proc. of the 1st ACM Conf. on Electronic Commerce (EC'99)*, 78–86, 1999.

[Mau96]   U. Maurer. Modelling a Public-Key Infrastructure. In *Proc. of the 4th European Symposium on Research in Computer Security (ESORICS'96)*, Lecture Notes in Computer Science vol. 1146, Springer-Verlag, 325–350, 1996.

[DIM02]   F. Di Vito, P. Inverardi, and G. Melideo. A context-aware approach to infer trust in Public Key Infrastructures. In *Proc. of the 17th IFIP World Computer Congress - International Workshop on Certification and Security in E-Services (CSES 2002)*, Kluwer Academic Publishers, 111–125, 2002.

[MPPW$^+$04]   G. Melideo, P. Penna, G. Proietti, R. Wattenhofer, and P. Widmayer. Truthful mechanisms for generalized utilitarian problems. In *3rd IFIP International Conference on Theoretical Computer Science (TCS'04)*, August 24-26, 2004, Toulouse, France. Proceedings will be published by Kluwer.

[NR99]   N. Nisan and A. Ronen. Algorithmic mechanism design. *Games and Economic Behaviour*, 35:166–196, 2001.

[NR00]   N. Nisan and A. Ronen. Computationally feasible VCG mechanisms. In *Proc. of the 2nd ACM Conference on Electronic Commerce (EC 2000)*, 242–252, 2000.

[Pap01]   C. H. Papadimitriou. Algorithms, games, and the Internet. In *Proc. of the 33rd Annual ACM Symposium on Theory of Computing (STOC'01)*, 749–753, 2001.

[SM97]   J. Su and D. Manchala. Building trust for distributed commerce transactions. In *Proc. of the 17th Int. Conf. Distributed Computing Systems*, IEEE CS Press, 322–329, 1997.

[Vic61]   W. Vickrey. Counterspeculation, auctions and competitive sealed tenders. *Journal of Finance*, 16:8–37, 1961.

A PREVENTION STRATEGY FOR SECURITY: A BAYESIAN APPROACH TO ANOMALIES DETECTION

Franco Arcieri and Andrea Dimitri
Nestor Laboratory
University of Rome "Tor Vergata", Italy
{arcieri, dimitri}@nestor.uniroma2.it

Abstract: Intrusion detection is one of the new frontiers in network security, but almost every implemented system is in trouble when it has to deal with new kind of attacks or when it has to give a real time response to predefined attacks. In this work, we assert that the way of improving intrusion detection is to consider the semantic aspects of the communication protocols. Furthermore, we analyze an intrusion detection model that tries to reach this goal putting together database logical design rules and new rules from Bayesian reasoning. In the final section, we sketch some application of the model and we show how to implement the model and how to face existing attacks using the model itself.

1.   INTRODUCTION

Network Intrusion Detection is the process of identification of malicious behaviours that damage a network and its resources. Intrusion Detection systems are usually classified in misuse-based and anomaly-based.

Solutions using misuse-based techniques contain a certain number of attack descriptions, called "signatures". When these systems recognize a signature instance in the data flows audited, they judge it as an attack. The positive characteristic of the misuse-based systems is that they usually generate very few false alarms, the negative one is that they recognize only previously defined attacks (the "signatures").

The anomaly–based techniques follow a complementary approach: they are based on models or profiles that capture the "normal" behaviour of a system. When something in the data flows is different from those models or profiles, they judge it as an attack. As known in literature, these systems are able to identify new attacks with unknown patterns, causing many false alarms.

For these reasons, both misuse-base systems and anomaly-based systems are not so frequently used: the system manager and the security manager have to cooperate every time to classify anomalous network events distinguishing real attacks from not dangerous behaviours. It is therefore evident that anomaly-based techniques depend exclusively from the ability to define their underlying models/profiles.

The challenge is to build a model that allows adding, within itself, rules and semantics that do not belong only to a static, predefined data set.

In that sense, some intrusion detection systems provide a sort of semantic functionalities in the Protocol Anomaly Filters: these filters search for a bad use of a communication protocol, according to the standard protocol rules.

An existing example of semantic based anomaly detection system is the human immune system.

The goal of the immune system of an organism is to defend it against harmful diseases and infections. The immune system is virtually able to recognize any foreign cell or molecule and eliminating it from the body. To do this, the immune system performs an operation of pattern recognition, with the perspective to distinguish molecules and cells of the body (called "self") from foreign ones (called "nonself"), potentially dangerous. The architecture of the immune system is multilayered, with defense systems provided in every one of the levels. The outmost layer, the skin, is the first barrier against infections. A second barrier is physiological: there are conditions such as pH and temperature that provide inappropriate living conditions for some foreign organisms (pathogens). Once pathogens have entered the body, they are handled with two types of approach: the innate immune system and the adaptive immune system. Examples of the first defense system are macrophages, that circulate in the organism and eat extra cellular molecules and foreign materials cleaning the body. Nevertheless, the most sophisticated system is the second one. It is called "adaptive" because it is responsible for immunity that is adaptively acquired during lifetime of the organism. Because the adaptive immune system provides the most potential from a computer security viewpoint, we will focus on it. The adaptive immune system can be viewed as a distributed detection system. It is constituted primarily of white blood cells, called lymphocytes. These small independent detectors circulate through the body in the blood and the lymph systems. They are negative detectors, because they act against foreign patterns, ignoring self patterns. Detection or recognition is caused by the affinity of the receptor that covers the surface of the lymphocyte and the pathogens. Detection is approximate: hence, a lymphocyte will bind with several different kinds of (structurally related) pathogens. To recognize most different pathogens is required a huge diversity of lymphocyte receptors and a great number of them. This diversity is partly achieved by generating lymphocyte receptors through a genetic process that introduces a huge amount of randomness. Even if receptors are randomly generated, in the organism there are not enough lymphocytes to provide a complete coverage of the space of all pathogen patterns. One estimate is that there are 10^8 different lymphocyte receptors in the body at any given time, which must detect potentially 10^16 different foreign patterns. To address this problem, the immune system has several mechanisms that make it dynamic and specific. Protection is made dynamic by the continual circulation of lymphocytes through the body and by a continual turnover of the lymphocyte population. The life of lymphocytes is typically a few days: the random renovation process will replace them by new ones. Dynamic protection increases the coverage provided by the immune system over time: the longer a pathogen is present in the body, the more likely it will be detected because it will meet a greater diversity of lymphocytes. Protection is made more specific by mechanism of learning and by memory. If the immune system detects a pathogen that it has not encountered before, it undergoes a primary response, during which it "learns" the structure of the specific pathogen, i.e. it evolves a set of lymphocytes with high affinity for that pathogen, through a process called affinity maturation. Affinity maturation produces a large number of lymphocytes that have high affinity for a particular pathogen, which accelerates its detection and elimination. Speed of response is important in the immune system because most pathogens are replicating and will cause increasing damage as their numbers increase. Last remark, each individual in a population has his tribe of lymphocytes, specific for each individual and different from another individual. This diversity of immune systems across a population greatly enhances the survival of the population as a whole.

Another reference that is similar to our approach could be the observation of a behaviour model. Let us suppose to observe a network security expert when he analyses outputs of some documentation system (router and firewall logs, sniffer output, ...) with the goal to discover network anomalies. He has in his mind a rule system that comes from his experience and from his background knowledge. This system is updated continuously because the expert continuously observes the world around him. When a network pattern does not match with one of the rules of his system, the expert starts a more detailed observation activity around the non-matching event.

2.   THE MODEL

In the context of Protocol Anomaly Detection is often said that most attacks are violations of the rules that define a protocol. This statement must be understood in a general context: let recall the DOS (denial of service) attack, that is based on a rapid succession of TCP connect operations. A TCP connect operation, not followed by other TCP operations, it is not a wrong operation in the context of the TCP protocol: we can assert that it is an anomalous operation. Some times no other TCP operations follow a TCP connect because the other peer of the connection cannot complete his work session. In addition, well-known worms or backdoors are difficult to recognize as TCP protocol violations.

An attack is a violation of an expected behaviour. This behaviour must be defined in a rule system.

Starting from this definition, we will build our model. We want to refer to a more general context: the context of the relational model. The relational model allows us to design complex scenarios. Network attacks, when they are not only simple service negation, are made by complex phases that cross the communication protocol stack. Therefore, to design complex scenarios we use the tools of the relational model. This model has a drawback: it hasn't tools to manage the semantic of the world we are representing, in particular, the semantic of the tuple to be inserted in the database. The logical design of databases and, in particular, the integrity constraint theory, could support us facing this limit. In this way we add the network rules to our model. However, this is not enough; the next step is to extend the classical concept of integrity constraint. To obtain this, we will use solutions deriving from Bayesian reasoning.

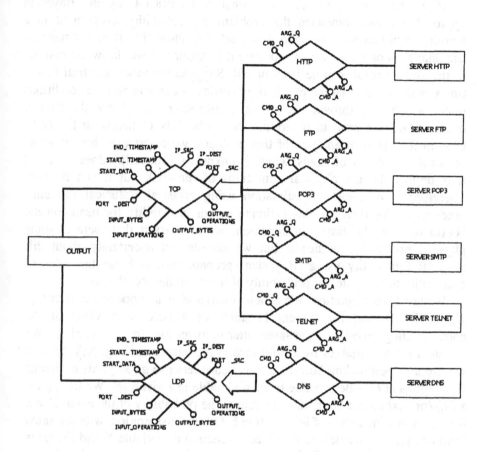

2.1   Bayesian reasoning

In a nutshell, the Bayesian probability of an event x is a person's degree of belief in that event (subjective approach). Whereas in classical approach probability is a physical property of the world (e.g. the probability that a coin will land heads) in the Bayesian approach probability is a property of the person who assigns it. Here we want to notate that the Bayesian approach doesn't neglect the classical one. When assigning a probability to an event of flip of a coin, a person can take in account only physical properties of the context of the flip. The classical concept of probability can become the starting point for building a Bayesian probabilistic model. But in the model have to enter also other source of knowledge, such as prior knowledge and historical information.

If we have a dataset that we consider significant, by the Bayesian approach we can transform the problem of probability assignment in a learning problem starting from a dataset. To show this fact, consider an irregular coin or a coin we are not sure it is regular. If we throw the coin up in the air, the result can be head or tail. Suppose we repeat the trial N + 1 times, making sure that the physical properties of the coin and the conditions under which it is thrown out remain stable over time. From the first N observations, we want to determine the probability of heads on the N-1h toss. In the classical analysis of this problem, we assert that there is some physical probability of heads, which is unknown. Probability does exist and it is defined by the physical conditions of the trial, but it is unknown. Therefore it is object of estimation using classical statistical inference procedures. We then use this estimate as our probability for heads on the N+1th toss. In the Bayesian approach, we also assert that there is some physical probability of heads, but we encode out uncertainty about this physical probability using (Bayesian) probabilities, and use the rules of probability to compute our probability of heads on the N+1th toss.

We need some notation. We denote a variable by an upper-case letter (eg. X; Y;X_i; Θ), and the current instance, or a state or a value of the corresponding variable by the same letter in lower case (e.g., x; y; x_i; θ). We denote a set of variables by a bold-face upper-case letter (e.g. $\mathbf{X}$;$\mathbf{Y}$;$\mathbf{X_i}$) and we use a corresponding bold-face lower-case letter (e.g., $\mathbf{x}$; $\mathbf{y}$; $\mathbf{x_i}$) to denote an assignment of state or value to each variable in a given set. We use $p(X = x / \xi)$ (or $p(x/ \xi)$ as a shorthand) to denote the probability of the event $X = x$ for a person with a state of information ξ. Other consideration, with the same formulas $p(x / \xi)$ we denote the density function of variable X and the mass or cumulative function $F(X)$. Whether $p(x / \xi)$ refers to a probability, a probability density or a probability distribution will be clear from the contest.

Let's return to the irregular coin problem. Let Θ to be the variable whose values θ correspond to the possible true value of the physical probability of the event heads. The probability θ is a random variable and we express the uncertainty about Θ with the density function $p(\theta/ \xi)$. In addition, we use X_l to denote the variable representing the outcome of the l-th toss, for $l = 1,\ldots\ldots,N + 1$, and $D = \{X_1=x_1, \ldots\ldots X_N = x_N \}$ to denote the set of our observations.

Thus, in Bayesian terms, the irregular coin problem reduces to computing $p(x_{N+1}/D, \xi)$ from $p(\theta/ \xi)$. To do so, we first use Bayes theorem to obtain the probability distribution for Θ given D and background knowledge ξ:

$$p(\theta|D,\xi) = \frac{p(\theta|\xi)\ p(D|\theta,\xi)}{p(D|\xi)}$$

where

$$p(D|\xi) = \int p(D|\theta,\xi)\ p(\theta|\xi)\ d\theta$$

p(D/ θ, ξ) is the convergence point between the classical approach and the Bayesian approach. For the conditions of the trials we have a binomial distribution:

$$p(D/ \theta,\ \xi) = \theta(1-\theta)$$

therefore first equation becomes

$$p(\theta|D,\xi) = \frac{p(\theta|\xi)\ \theta^h\ (1-\theta)^t}{p(D|\xi)}$$

where h and t are the number of heads and tails observed in D, respectively. p(θ / ξ) is the prior probability and p(θ /D,ξ) is the posterior probability, the effective object of dispute between classics and Bayesians. The quantities h and t are said to be sufficient statistics for binomial distribution. Finally, we average over the possible values of Θ (using the expansion rule of probability) to determine the probability that the N+1th toss of the coin will come up heads:

$$p(X_{N+1} = heads|D,\xi) = \int p(X_{N+1} = heads|\theta,\xi)\ p(\theta|D,\xi)\ d\theta$$

$$= \int \theta\ p(\theta|D,\xi)\ d\theta \equiv E_{p(\theta|D,\xi)}(\theta)$$

where E means expectation or average, and p(θ / D,ξ) is the weight element.

To complete the exposure we have to spend some world about the prior probability p(Θ/ ξ). In the Bayesian approach this is a predefined input. One possible way is to get a standard distribution with some known properties.

Another way is the complete building of the probability distribution by a predefined knowledge state. We will see that in our model prior probability distribution is a basic concept. Prior distribution is often ignored where can become the right tool to introduce rules in a intrusion detection system.

Let's start to see how the above exposure enter in our model. In the field of logic design of a database there is the key declaration phase. A set of attribute is a key for a given entity set. We can try to review the key concept in the Bayesian approach. Generally speaking, for a given set of attributes X, parameter θ that includes the fact that the given set is a key set for the database, is a Boolean variable. If X is really a key $\theta = 1$; in the other case $\theta = 0$. In the Bayesian world θ become Θ; it is a random variable. An example: we take into consideration a teacher having an exam session. In the universe of persons, Name and Surname aren't a key attribute set. Supposing that in the same exam session arrive three persons with the same Name and Surname. This fact can become suspicious for the teacher. This last statement tells us that in the mind of the teacher {Name, Surname} could be a sort of key.

2.2 Generalized integrity constraints

2.2.1 Domain constraints

Every attribute or set of attributes has to be linked with a domain of possible values. This is the most elementary form of integrity constraint. But it is very important in the field of network information systems.

In the Bayesian world, in the space of admitted values for the domain we have to build a probability distribution. Almost every attack can be identified by some of its steps that are violation of one or more integrity constraints. We can think at backdoors, or various forms of worm viruses, or techniques that use man in the middle attacks to intermediate a communication.

2.2.2 Functional dependencies

It is easy to translate the concept of functional dependence in the direction of the concept of probabilistic dependence, and Bayesian inference methods supply all needed tools to express this new type of dependence.

Some observations can be done about the DOS attack. We want to demonstrate that DOS attack does not agree with the following two constraints: IP→TCP-CONNECTION and TCP-SEND→TCP-CONNECT. Consider the first functional dependence: in the TCP protocol the tuple (client ip, server ip, client service, server service) represents, at a given time, a key tuple for the TCP connection. In a static Local Area Network there are not two connections having the same key tuple. We said that in our Bayesian world this tuple is a random variable Θ(client ip, server ip, client service, server service). Seen as an event, the fact of to be or not to be a key it is a trivial random variable, because it takes value "true" with probability 1. But we can study the random variable Θ(client ip) at a given time. In this way, we formalize the fact that in some DOS attacks there are many open connections starting from the same ip address.

To better understand the second functional dependence violation, we will introduce the Bayesian concept of *explaining away*. Consider this simple probabilistic graph:

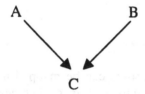

There are two causes A and B that compete to explain the effect C. Note that variables A and B are marginally independent but conditionally dependent. In terms of probabilities we have

$$P(A/B,C) \,!= P(A)$$

This is known as Berkson paradox or *explaining away*.

Let us return to the DOS attack. In the TCP protocol, we have the functional dependency SEND→TCP-CONNECT. A TCP send operation functionally implies a TCP connect operation. In other words, the send operation is one of the possible effects of the TCP connect operation. Following the Bayesian approach we can assert that in the HTTP protocol, the WEB client/server protocol, TCP connect is the cause and TCP send is the effect. This means that, considering the *explaining away* concept, two TCP connect operations are independent *a priori*, but they become dependent *a posteriori* because a TCP send operation follows all TCP connect operations. In other words, a connect event is bound to the final result of the other previous TCP connection: a dialogue cannot continue if the present phases are not going ok. A large number of TCP connect without TCP send, in a client/server protocol is a clear signal of network anomalies.

2.2.3   Generalized Functional dependencies

In the field of logical db modeling, there are many types of constraints or dependencies (multi-valued dependencies, inclusion dependencies, ...). In a more general context, we introduce the concept of generalized functional dependencies. The basic feature of all forms of constraint says: if there are some tuples in the instance, then there are also other tuples, or some components of these tuples have some features. Using first order logic we can assert that a constraint is a sentence of form:

$$\Box x1...\Box xn\ [\varphi(x1....xn) \rightarrow \Box z1...zk\ \psi(y1...ym)]$$

where $\{z1...zk\} = \{y1...ym\}-\{x1....xn\}$ and where φ is a atoms conjunction, possibly empty.

2.2.4   Probabilistic graphs

All above showed constraints can be mapped in the Bayesian world by the concept of probabilistic graph or Bayesian network.

A Bayesian network for a set of variables $X = \{X1,............,Xn\}$ consists of (1) a network structure S that encodes a set of conditional independence assertions about variables in X, and (2) a set P of local probability distributions associated with each variable. Together, these components define the joint probability distribution for X. The network structure S is a directed acyclic graph. The nodes in S are in one-to-one correspondence with the variables X. We use Xi to denote both the variable and its corresponding node, and Pai to denote the parents of node Xi in S as well as the variables corresponding to those parents. The lack of possible arcs in S encodes conditional independencies. In particular, given the structure S, the joint probability distribution for X is given by

$$p(\mathbf{x}) = \prod_{i=1}^{n} p(x_i|\mathbf{pa}_i)$$

The local probability distributions P are the distributions corresponding to the terms in the product of the above equation. Consequently, the pair (S; P) encodes the joint distribution p(x).

In our context, we refer to a probabilistic graph as a GIC (generalized integrity constraint).

2.2.5   Two layer, probabilistic model

A probabilistic model can be introduced as:

$$M = \{ \; \Omega, \; \text{ß}(\Omega), m(\text{ß}(\Omega)) \}$$

where Ω is an event space, $\text{ß}(\Omega)$ is an algebra in that space and m is a probabilistic measure in the algebra. With a mapping between a semantic model (the logical model) and the Bayesian definition of probability we have introduced a probabilistic model. Explicitly:

$$M = \{ \; [DS], \; [DAG \; over \; DS], \; m \}$$

DS = Database Schema
DAG over DS = Direct Acyclic Graph over the database schema
m = probabilistic measure over [DAG over DS].

We introduce another derived model:

$$M' = \{ [DAG \; over \; DS], \; \text{ß}([DAG \; over \; DS]), \; m' \}$$

We have to explain in more details m and m'. For m construction we take in account Bayesian learning methods. For m' construction we consider a concept borrow from information theory.

2.2.6   Learning Probabilities in a Bayesian Network

In literature there are many source about this problem. Here we want just recall them (see bibliography) and recall principles about the problem. Methodology in learning probabilities for a Bayesian network is that of refining a defined prior distribution with other source of information. For example data capturing with an advanced sniffer.

We fix now two aspects, first one: the prior probability means rules. If a DAG represents a protocol or a work section, we know rules about it and we state that rules in the form of prior probabilities.

Second aspect: in our world we have simple DAG. We have many simple DAG. An open problem in the classical approach to IDS is the complexity to learn one big abstract and only historic model. Many data, a big dataset but many difficulties to work with it. An opposite approach is to have many small rules an to try to match them progressively.

2.2.7   A model in DAG space

The need of a model in DAG space and not only in event space, rises because we are building a dynamic model. To show this dynamism we need a correlation measure in DAG space. To do this we have to borrow some concepts from information theory.

Definition 1 (Information Gap) Let P=(p1,....,pk) and Q=(q1,.......,qk) two probability distributions. Information delay between P and Q is defined as follows:

$$D(Q/P) = \sum p_i \log(p_i/q_i)$$

Conventionally we set $0*\log(0)=0$. In particular:

$$0 \leq D(Q/P) \leq \infty$$

$$D(Q/P) = 0 \leftrightarrow P \equiv Q$$

$$D(Q/P) = \infty \leftrightarrow \square i \ t.. \ q_i = 0$$

$$D(Q/P) \neq D(P/Q)$$

Definition 2 (Mutual Information) The information gap between the join probability distribution Pxy and the distribution PxPy is the mutual information between X and Y.

$$I(X/Y) = D(Pxy/PxPy)$$

Mutual information can be viewed as a measure of conditional dependence between variables X and Y. So we have I(X/Y)=0 if Pxy = Px*Py. Mutual information is symmetric in variables exchange. In information theory two variables are dependent if they exchange information. This a dynamic view of variables correlation.

Another important concept is the auto- mutual information, i.e. the mutual information of X and X.

$$P(x_i, x_j) = 0 \text{ if } I \mathrel{!}= j$$

$$P(x_i, x_i) = x_i$$

So we have:

$$I(X/X) = \sum p_{ij} \log(p_{ij}/p_i \, p_j) = - \sum p_i \log(p_i).$$

Auto mutual information is called Shannon entropy.

Definition 3 (DAGs Mutual Information) The mutual information between two DAGs is the max mutual information between all couples of nodes one for DAG.

So we define m' as the DAG Mutual Information. We shall see that when we will explain model dynamic we will use DAGs Mutual Information concept and entropy concept. Return to immune systems. They have a mechanism to generate new lymphocytes in a normal situation (dynamism), and a mechanism to front an attack (specialization). The concept of entropy allows to generate random GIC; only those GIC with a small entropy will be considered valid, i. e. GIC that reflects the semantic of the model. The concept of DAGs Mutual Information introduces a metric in the space of DAGs, so when an event doesn't correspond to a gived DAG, the system will analyze near DAGs.

3.   APPLICATIONS

3.1   Sniffers

We must have an proper environment allowing to start with design. The input database and its structure defines what we could build over it and subsequently, what type of surveys we could do. The great advantage of our approach is that we developed our analysis starting from a robust platform that is database designing tool. But this is true if there exists a tool allowing to write in the designed DBMS. Common sniffer or common log files can't develop this job. Lab Nestor developed an environment to do this. The tool is not only a sniffer but a protocol recognizer and rebuilder so that it can be used to insert directly output data in the planned database.

3.2   IDS system organization

The designed IDS is a global filter in Database insert query. An insert query starts with a network event. Before the insert step can start IDS verify all its constraints. There are two other aspects to focus. First, there is a parallel task that refresh continually the constraints set. It builds new constraint proposal, validates it with the current set of constraint (coherence check) and the current historical data and, if the validation step is ok, puts it in the constraints set. It review old constraints to validate their current validity. Second, if the system locates a constraint violation, it starts a new task of generation of adjacent constraints and check with data object of violation. Concepts introduced in the below section define how all this operations can be achieved.

3.3 IDS configuration steps

The crucial step in the configuration phase is the constraints definition. There is a set of constraint that depends on the rules of the networks. In this case we refer to classical constraints. For the other part of the constraints we can consider three step: protocols analysis, work sessions analysis and applications analysis. We remember that we have to state rules; habits are an output of the model. So the rule is: "usually there is a DNS request and after an HTTP request". The model learns that the host name of DNS answer and host called in HTTP request are the same. Then, this type of event sequences are regular, other different types of sequences are to be validated.

3.4 Attacks

Every attack is a violation of a constraint, but a crucial point is that we have to consider where the violation is located. Many attacks have a first step concerning substitution of an host with another one. We are thinking at many types of TCP protocol violations, at Mitnick attack, at idle scanning, at some types of man in the middle attacks. In all this cases violation is located in the client network. If IDS is located in server network to protect final services locations, then we note nothing. If an intruder extorts a password from the PC of a regular user, floods this PC and manages TCP connection in its PC, there are many violations but they all are client side. From the Server side is all regular. Security is a complex task and an organization task. IDS has to be a part of a system.

Here we can state that we built our IDS on a robust platform and this is important. There are many studies in functional dependencies and implication problem that define environment where a set of constraints is complete and close. In our world we can state exactly what we are looking, and what we aren't.

4. CONCLUSIONS

The main goal of this paper is to explain how to add semantic in the field of IDS and how this is a crucial step in the perspective of adding learning in IDS. The approach we follow has many differences from the standard one.

We start from an existing and robust model, that is conceptual and logic database design. All development in this field can potentially be translated in the IDS field. Future works could analyze the implication problem and the goal to define a model sound and complete. An IDS can't continue to be thought as an oracle that, given a network event, output an answer. Every IDS has to be characterized with its limits and properties.

Prior knowledge strongly enters in the firsts phase of designing. This is true because we have a concept of constraint simple, so every prior information it is easily introduced in our model.

The output of the designing phase is a set of simple constraints, a set that is refreshed during the life of IDS.

Another important feature of our proposal is in its dynamism facing a constraint violation. Rarely an attack is something of punctual and when it is punctual cannot be really dangerous. A final attack is a process and the true goal of an IDS is to understand it. Introducing a metric in the network space is a step in this direction. We formalized a new concept of network as interconnected system. This is the base to do complete intrusion detection. Only in this direction we can avoid the problem of false alarms.

References

[Coh87]   F. Cohen Computer viruses. Computers & Security, 6:22-35,1987.

[FHS96] S. Forrest, S. Hofmeyr, A. Somayaji. Computer immunology. Communications of the ACM (Dec. 1996).

[Hec96] D. Heckerman, A tutorial on learning with Bayesian networks, Microsoft Research tech. report, MSR-TR-95-06, 1996.

[Das01] K. Das, Protocol Anomaly Detection for Network-based Intrusion Detection, GSEC, 2001.

[AGNT01] F. Arcieri, R. Giaccio, E. Nardelli, M. Talamo. A framewok for Inter-Organizational Public Administration Network Services. Proc. Of International Conference Advances in Infrastructures for Electronic Business, Science, and Education on the Internet (SSGRR 2001), L'Aquila, August 2001.

[Axe00] S. Axelsson, Intrusion Detection Systems: A taxonomy and Survey, Technical Report No 99-15, Dept of Computer Engineering. Chalmers University of Technology, Sweden, March 2000.

[DuM]   W. DuMouchel, Computer Intrusion Detection Based on Bayes Factors for Comparing Command Transition Probabilities, AT&T Labs, Research.

MOBILE FINANCIAL INFORMATION SERVICES, SECURITY, AND CERTIFICATION

Jan Muntermann, Heiko Roßnagel, Kai Rannenberg
Chair of Mobile Commerce and Multilateral Security
Johann Wolfgang Goethe-University Frankfurt
Graefstrasse 78

Tel. +49-69-798-25307
Fax +49-69-798-25306

D-60054 Frankfurt / Main, Germany
www.whatismobile.de

Abstract: *Non-institutional investors are normally unable to react quickly to market events, which can have significant impact on their portfolio value. Especially when a critical market event occurs much depends on processing the information efficiently and in time. Mobile information services may then improve the information supply for these investors. In this contribution we will determine which financial information services are suitable for mobile use and show what kind of improvements the use of this technology will provide. We take a look at the potential benefits of mobile financial information pull and push services and also determine the security requirements of such services comparing them with what current technology has to offer. It shows that none of the technologies used today is able to provide the support for all the stated security requirements and that at least three areas would profit from certification.*

Keywords: Mobile Commerce, E-Finance, Mobile Brokerage, Security Requirements

1. INTRODUCTION

The dynamic stock market developments of the last years showed that staying up to date with regard to financial information is of paramount importance. Otherwise investing in stock markets loses its attractiveness [FoRe03]. Therefore an automated supply of personalized and decision relevant information, independent from time and the location of the investor is needed. While demand-oriented web-based information services such as observation and alerting systems have improved the information supply for investors [LooCha02], these traditional client/server systems can not provide time and location independent services. Therefore these infrastructures are not appropriate for an automated delivery of time critical financial information. In particular for non-institutional investors, who are unable to track all relevant market events, mobile financial information services can help reducing reaction time and moving these investors on a level playing field with the institutional investors. Mobile information services allow real-time information delivery and can heavily cut reaction time to market events, e.g. bad market news published as company announcement. The growing availability of powerful mobile devices and new wireless data services (e.g. GPRS) is enhancing the availability and affordability of mobile financial information services. Since the transferred information is the basis for initiating and blocking high-volume monetary transactions (or at least for influencing them), a high level of security is needed, e.g. to prevent attackers from spying, suppressing, or manipulating information. The goal of this paper is to show which type of financial information services are suitable for mobile usage and how these services might be implemented. We then focus on how to secure these services adequately and on how they are secured currently. Section 2 provides an overview on financial information services and their usage in mobile environments. Section 3 discusses the security requirements of these services as well as the level of security provided by market-available technologies. Section 4 concludes our findings and gives an outlook on future work and the need for certification.

2. MOBILIZED FINANCIAL INFORMATION SERVICES

2.1 Financial Aspects

By allocating securities, investors diversify their portfolio and choose the most appropriate ratio of risky and less-risky assets [ElmKi03]. This allocation aims at an efficient ratio of potential returns versus risks taken. Therefore investors require powerful real-time information services. This need increases if the portfolios contain various risky and volatile assets.

Today so called "pull" and "push" *information services* are available, which require different information system infrastructures. Using pull services investors can request relevant market information to prepare decisions. Furthermore push services which are triggered by market events can deliver information in real-time. Based on the received information it might be advisable to reallocate portfolio positions quickly. This reallocation is done by selling and buying (new) assets and is supported by so-called *transaction services*. The availability of new, web-based I&C-systems in the area of information and transaction services has empowered non-institutional investors during the recent years. Even though, most of these systems cannot provide location independence for users needing information in optimal time.

Non-institutional investors are usually not able to analyze all portfolio relevant market information continuously, as they have more things to do than to watch monitors with stock quotes the whole day. They also are not professionally trained in quickly deciding which information is relevant to their investment decisions. Mobile information services enable location independence while personalized services help to filter the information flow.

2.2 Portfolio Observation

Portfolio observation services can be realized by monitoring market events and continuously analyzing the portfolio status based on criteria defined by the investor. The investor determines events to be monitored by e.g. defining static and dynamic price limits and also determines the preferred communication channel. For this configuration conventional web-based systems can be used, while the delivery of the notifications needs push services such as e-mail, Short Message Service or Multimedia Message Service.

However, portfolio observation comprises more than monitoring price limits. General market information that might be relevant for the portfolio development needs to be identified, selected, and delivered. Examples are personalized notifications in case of changing portfolio ratios (such as the stock quotes), financial metrics (e.g. changes in credit ratings), or market information (such as company announcements). All this might have major impact on the short-term development of shares, especially if published financial parameters do not comply with market expectations. This effect can be measured by comparing the price movement during the event period (e.g. the respective trading day) with the movement during another observation period (e.g. the trading days before) in which no critical market event occurred [MuMa04].

2.2.1 Added Value from Mobile Support

In general mobile portfolio observation enables faster reactions, especially through reduced delays for the delivery of information and through the delivery of personalized market information. The monitoring is usually realized by processes on backend-systems (application and database servers) at the online broker or the bank. The investor is informed via push services if a monitored event occurs.

In particular, the mobile enhancement in terms of information delivery makes portfolio observation a mission-critical and helpful asset. Relevant information can be the above-mentioned company announcements, in which companies publish e.g. quarterly financial data or news from their management board. This information may well cause abnormal price changes, especially if new information differs from market expectations [Graha62]. On the other hand for periodically calculated portfolio figures, that are usually calculated once a day, mobile push services are not required because the information content of these figures is of longer lifetime. In this case conventional web services are appropriate.

2.2.2 Technical Realization of Mobile Information Services

A well-known GSM Phase 1 Service offering push functionality is the Short Message Service (SMS). This service has been a market success in the last years, representing remarkable revenue for the companies providing the system infrastructure. However, one weakness of the SMS is that it does not guarantee delivery time. Version 2.0 of the Wireless Application Protocol (WAP) [WF01] defines a push service framework, which specifies protocols to transfer messages and documents to mobile devices within classic client/server environments. Although this framework was released in July 2001 appropriate push services are not yet available. The availability of mobile devices supporting WAP 2.0 did not change much of this situation. The WAP Forum has been substituted by the Open Mobile Alliance (OMA) in 2002, which already has released an extension of the previous push framework [OMA02]. This extension is able to process incoming e-mails through the so-called e-mail notification (EMN). This technology requires new mobile devices with EMN support and an installed conventional e-mail client which enables the device to download e-mails from conventional mail servers.

2.3   Portfolio Analysis

Besides providing share prices and calculating portfolio metrics the portfolio analysis assists investors to improve their investment decisions. Furthermore, it supports investors to identify positive and negative correlations of asset returns and risk measured in price variances. Portfolio analysis provides different types of information, which have different maturity. Some information doesn't change very often (e.g. assets of a balance sheet); some can only be calculated periodically due to high calculation complexity [Daco01]. Usually pull services are used for portfolio analysis, i.e. when the shareholder requires information about portfolio positions, after the portfolio monitoring service informed about a relevant market event.

2.3.1   Added Value from Mobile Support

Web-based portfolio analysis services are available for several years and have enormously improved the information supply for investors. To support long-term (strategic) investment decisions, web-based information services are appropriate. However the focus of mobile financial information services is to support investors' in urgent (intraday) investment decisions. Already the introduction of these web-based systems has reduced the possible decision horizon enormously. The timelines of sensitive investment decisions depend on risk attributes and on the availability of portfolio analysis systems [BoMe00]. When short-term information is needed (due to highly volatile asset classes) conventional web-based systems can not guarantee an adequate service. A basic analysis is the supply of current price information and the performance of the portfolio positions. If a situation demands a short-term shifting of portfolio positions, a calculation of optimal buying and selling volumes might help achieving a portfolio composition with an efficient ratio of risk and expected return. As such calculations require historic quote series [Shar66], it is sensible to do calculations on the application servers. Moreover new market forecasts or quarterly business figures may require a spontaneous research about a certain company. In this case the investor has to get a quick review of the most important financial statistics.

2.3.2   Technical Realization of Mobile Portfolio Analysis

In the mobile setting a wide range of services and system infrastructures can be used to realize a reasonable portfolio management. When much information is required an implementation via pull services is advisable, and this leads to the usage of WAP. WAP has been developed for GSM data services with their low data rates. The aim was to develop a protocol family, which allows to access documents on the internet. These documents have comparatively simple designs to keep the data volumes low. Although WAP could not meet expectations in terms of market penetration, it is useful for mobile portfolio analysis, as the lack of multimedia support is negligible.

3. SECURITY REQUIREMENTS OF MOBILE FINANCIAL INFORMATION SERVICES

3.1 General Security Requirements and Mobile Financial Information Services

Four general criteria [Rann00] can help to structure the security requirements on the mobile usage of suitable financial information services:

1. *Confidentiality*: Confidentiality is the protection from unauthorized disclosure of information to third parties. Those could be employees of the financial service provider, the mobile service provider or anyone else. Within the scope of mobile financial services this includes for example the protection of the user from exposing his financial situation or trading strategy to others.

2. *Availability*: Availability is the protection from unauthorized withholding of information or services, i.e. information services. It can be very damaging for an investor to get time-critical information delayed or not at all. Since financial information services could have a direct influence on possibly following transactions, the lack of availability of a service can cause a damage for the investor, e.g. if he fails to sell his declining stocks.

3. *Integrity*: Integrity protects the user from unauthorized manipulation of data or systems. It ensures the user that the data he receives hasn't been altered while being sent to him or while being on his device. False, modified or insufficient information might lead to wrong decisions and to financial losses. Since unauthorized manipulations can't be prevented in non-trusted environments, the integrity of the used data must be protected by all means necessary and breaches have to be detected and documented.

4. *Accountability*: Accountability defines the fact that actions or documents can be associated with the originator, who could be a person or company, so that they cannot deny transactions they made at a later date. After complaints from customers about misleading information or unauthorized transactions resulting in financial losses, one wants to be able to trace back the originator of the information or who has altered the transaction?

3.2 A Short Security Analysis of Mobile Financial Information Services

3.2.1 Portfolio Observation

In the area of portfolio observation individual messages on new events will be delivered by means of push technology. The level of security depends initially on the relevance of the portfolio respectively on the delivered message but also on the relevance the delivered message may have for the portfolio. For example, a limit message must have a high level of confidentiality as any information delivered to the investor would allow direct assessments of the investments in his portfolio. The information gained could be used directly against the investor by e.g. estimating discrepancies in his financial position and making those public. It could also be used indirectly as basis for an attack on the integrity of selected information e.g. modifying the information or forging it.

Ad hoc disclosures need less confidentiality than limit messages as not all ad-hoc messages the investor receives relate to titles in his portfolio. However, it could still be possible to some extent to draw conclusions on the content and titles contained in the portfolio. When general information and trends do not allow conclusions about the portfolio content or the investment strategy this information does not need to be treated in confidentially.

Missing availability of services in the push scenarios may result in serious consequences e.g. considerable financial losses if limit messages are delayed intentionally or by accident.

Preserving integrity is the prime objective for portfolio observation services, since they depend on the correctness of information. Accountability and the knowledge of the source of information are important, if decisions have to be made in short time and no second or third sources can be used.

3.2.2 Portfolio Analysis

If closely related to a specific portfolio, portfolio analysis does disclose quite a lot about the content as well as the trading strategy of the owner. Hence the confidentiality level depends on the requirements of the owner. The requirements related to integrity and accountability of a portfolio analysis increase with the importance of the decisions as a result of that portfolio analysis. The requirements on the integrity do increase the lesser the possibilities are (e.g. due to time constraints) to call for further analysis for comparison purposes. The availability requirements of portfolio analysis services depend on the actual need of the investor making decisions and how time critical these are.

3.3   Suitability of Used and Available Technology in Regards to Security

3.3.1   Short Message Service (SMS)

The Short Message Service (SMS) is an attractive option for financial service information providers. Here the data of the service information provider will be transmitted to the SMS service centre (usually a mobile communication provider). From there, it will be forwarded by (cable) data links and eventually delivered to the mobile device over the air. During this process the data is transmitted as plain text except during the wireless transmittal. Consequently the security target of confidentiality is not achieved without introduction of security measures at the user level [FuFri01].

Also a manipulation of data during the transfer over the various communication paths cannot be prevented or traced back by the investor. Moreover an effective identification of the originator of the message is not possible as the mobile phone number indicated on the SMS message can be easily manipulated in the SMS-centre. Offers about how to send SMS under any sender number can be found on the internet [Eton03].

A possible solution to this problem is the use of a suitable 'signature process' [Ran03] which is able to protect the integrity and accountability on application level. To enable this the mobile device needs specific software for the verification of signatures. This however is a major challenge due to the many different types of mobile devices. Similar problems occur if full confidentiality is required, e.g. via encryption on the application level from the initial source to the final recipient. Full availability of SMS-messages does not exist. There is no guarantee that messages will be delivered at all or that they will be delivered in time, since SMS messages are being delivered based on the load of the network (store-and-forward service) [Schi03, GSM01].

3.3.2   WAP

WAP 1.x uses WTLS, a security protocol based on SSL, to improve the confidentiality and reliability of data during transmittal [Schi03]. The WTLS protocol supports primarily the security objectives of accountability, confidentiality and integrity. However, a problem exists if the WAP-server is not installed in the protected area of the financial information service provider and is connected directly to the infrastructure of the mobile communication provider. In that case end-to-end security will get lost at the place where the WAP-Gateway does decrypt the data. [FuFri01]. WAP 2.0 uses TLS to secure the communication and ensures real end-to-end security. However, only a few devices support TLS [cf. 2.2].

3.3.3   Web-based solutions

Especially the integration of PDAs and mobile phones offers new perspectives for mobile financial service providers. New mobile devices have web browsers able to encrypt the data transmitted by means of SSL. This enables a real "end-to-end" security during the transmission. The integrity and authenticity of the data can be achieved by means of digital signatures, provided suitable programs are available on the user platform (device) [Ran03]. With web-based solutions all security requirements can be fulfilled provided that the service providers as well as the mobile device do support the relevant protection technology.

4.   CONCLUSION AND FUTURE WORK

The mobile financial information services introduced provide advantages for investors as well as for service providers: The timely and location independent delivery of time critical market information improves the level of information of investors, which may result in improved investment decisions. From the view of providers of mobile financial information services the upgraded service quality and service personalisation may improve customer relations. The security requirements for mobile financial information services are rising with the specialization and personalization of the required information and also with a reduction of the time between the receipt of information and need for decisions. Current applications do not or not yet comply with the security requirements. They still need to be enhanced by encryption and signature procedures as well as by redundancy concepts at the user level. In at least three areas certification would be useful:
1. Does the mobile device display the content correctly? This would be a certification towards the investor using the Common Criteria [ISO1999] and being paid by the device manufacturer or communication provider.
2. Does the SIM produce correct signatures? This would be a certification towards the investor and broker using the Common Criteria [ISO1999] being paid by the SIM manufacturer or communication provider.

3. Does the SIM represent a liable investor? This would be a certification towards the broker, using e.g. a signature certificate according to the EU directive. Payment for this would have to come from the investor or the communication provider – the latter to encourage mobile brokerage and the related traffic.

5.   REFERENCES

[BoMe00] Bodie, Z.; Merton. R. C.: Finance, Upper Saddle River, New Jersey, 2000.

[Daco01] Dacorogna, M.; Gençay, R.; Müller, U.; Olsen, R.; Pictet, O.: An Introduction to High-Frequency Finance, San Diego, Califonia, 2001.

[Dorn01] Dornan, A.: The Essential Guide to Wireless Communications Applications – From Cellular Systems to WAP and M-Commerce, Upper Saddle River 2001.

[ElmKi03] Elmiger, G.; Kim, S.S.: RiskGrade Your Investments, Hoboken, New Jersey 2003.

[Eton03] e-tones.co.uk: „Anonymous SMS", www.e-tones.co.uk/index.php?cpid=31, [2003-06-14].

[EU_esig1999] European Union: DIRECTIVE 1999/93/EC OF THE EUROPEAN PARLIAMENT AND OF THE COUNCIL of 13 December 1999 on a Community framework for electronic signatures.

[FoRe03] Forrester Research: Eurpean Online Finance's Quit Boom, Cambridge, 2003.

[FuFri01] Fuchß, T.; Fritsch, L.: Endgeräte für den M-Commerce: Defizite und Aussichten, in KES 1, Ingelheim 2001, 6-8.

[Graha62] Graham, B.; Dodd, D. L.; Cottle, S.: Security Analysis – Principles and Technique, 4th Ed., New York 1962.

[GSM01] GSM Association: Identification of Quality of Service aspects of popular Services (GSM and 3G), Version 3.0.0, www.gsmworld.com/documents/ireg/ir41.pdf, 2001, [2003-06-08].

[GSM03]   GSM   Association: MMS   –   What   is   MMS?, www.gsmworld.com/technology/mms/whatis_mms.shtml, 2003 [2003-05-28].

[ISO1999] Evaluation Criteria for IT Security, Parts 1-3; International Standard 15408; 1999

[LooCha02] Looney, C. A.; Chatterjee, D.: Web-Enabled Transformation of the Brokerage Industrie. In: Communications of the ACM, 45 (3), 2002.

[MuMa04] Muntermann, J.: Notifying Investors in Time - A Mobile Information System Approach, Proceedings of the 10th Americas Conference on Information Systems (AMCIS'2004); New York, August 2004

[OMA02]   Open   Mobile   Alliance: E-Mail   Notification   Version   1.0. www.openmobilealliance.org/ omacopyrightNEW.asp?doc=OMA-EMN-v1_0-20021031-C.zip, 2002, [2003-07-10].

[Ran03] Ranke, J.; Fritsch, L.; Rossnagel, H.: M-Signaturen aus rechtlicher Sicht. Datenschutz und Datensicherheit 27 , Wiesbaden 2003, 95-100.

[Rann00] Rannenberg, K.: Multilateral Security – A concept and examples for balanced security. Proc. 9th ACM New Security Paradigms WS 2000, Cork, Ireland, 151-162.

[Schi03] Schiller, J.: Mobile Communications,2nd Edition, London 2003.

[Shar66] Sharpe, W. F.: Mutual Fund Performance. Journal of Business, 1966, 39 (1),119-138.

[StraAna03] Strategy Analytics: Global Cellular Data Forecasts (2003 - 2008), 2003.

[WapFo01] WAP Forum: WAP Push Architectural Overview, Version 03-Jul-2001. www1.wapforum.org/tech/documents/WAP-250-PushArchOverview-20010703-a.pdf, 2001, [2003-02-12].

H/W BASED FIREWALL FOR HIGH-PERFORMANCE NETWORK SECURITY

Jong-Gook Ko, Ki-Young Kim and Keul-Woo Ryu
Electronics and Telecommunications Research Institute (ETRI)
1 Kajeong-dong, Yuseong-gu, Daejeon 305-350, Korea
Tel +82-42-860-5940, Fax +82-42-861-5611
{jgko, kykim, kwryu}@etri.re.kr

Abstract: Recently, enterprises, service provider, and e-businesses confront increasing security and performance challenges. Securing network, host, and on-line application is absolutely important. At the same time, security function must not disturb productivity. To ensure that increasing network traffic is safe and their networks are secure, these organizations must provide security with bias toward solutions that accommodate performance demands, while providing the security and networking features required to run their businesses. That is, best solutions are those that combine high performance with topnotch security. For satisfying those requirements, we have developed hardware based and high performance Security Gateway System (SGS) which providing security functions such Firewall, IDS, Rate-limiting, and Traffic metering in wire speed. In this paper, we especially describe how H/W based Firewall features are implemented in SGS.

Key words: Firewall, Network Security, Security Gateway System, packet filtering

1.   INTRODUCTION

Today, Firewall among many security functions is essentially provided in all security system. It means that firewall is fundamental and important security function. When a network is connected to the Internet, its users are enabled to reach and communicate with the outside world. At the same time, however, the outside world can reach and interact with the network. In this dangerous situation, intermediate system can be located between the network and the Internet to establish a controlled link, and to erect an outer security wall or perimeter. The aim of this perimeter is to protect the network or hosts from threats and attacks. In short, firewall builds blockade between an internal network that is assumed to be secure and trusted, and another network, usually an external network, such as the Internet, that is not assumed to be secure and trusted. The general reasoning behind firewall usage is that without a firewall, a network's systems are more exposed to inherently insecure Internet protocols and corresponding services, as well as probes and attacks from hosts elsewhere on the Internet. Firewalls filter the traffic exchanged between networks, enforcing each network's access control policy. Firewalls ensure that only authorized traffic passes into and out of each connected network. To avoid compromise, the firewall itself must be hardened against attack. To enable security policy design and verification, a firewall must also provide strong monitoring and logging.

Network speeds have increased faster and faster in the last several years. Some networks run at gigabit speeds today, while 100-megabit networks have been commonplace. Even Internet connectivity speeds have increased to the point where 100 megabits is common at hosting sites, and is also becoming feasible for large organizations. Recently, 1giga, 2.5giga, even 10giga interfaces are developed and on the market.

The firewall technologies required to control inbound and outbound traffic have not, until now, developed as rapidly as networking speeds. The most popular firewall appliances today rely on desktop PC hardware and are implemented in software based, which can limit their performance. High-performance firewalls must surpass these limitations, and should be capable of performing more that simple security duties.

In this paper, we describe hardware based firewall which providing security function and assuring high performance. The rest of this paper is organized as follows. Section 2 describes design and composition of hardware based firewall. Performance test results are contained in section 3. And Conclusion and future work are discussed in section 4.

2.   SYSTEM DESIGN AND COMPOSITION

Hardware based and high performance Security Gateway System (SGS) provide security functions such as firewall, IDS, Rate-limiting, and traffic metering which are implemented on two FPGA (Xilinx Vertex II Pro) chips in each security board module. Security board also has embedded CPU MPC 860 that embedded Linux OS operating in. Total five security boards can be installed to SGS. Figure 1 depicts overall security board composition.

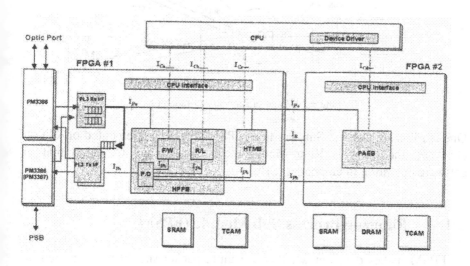

Figure 1: SGS secrity board composition

Firewall, Rate-limiting, and traffic metering are implemented in FPGA #1. and High Packet Processing Block(HPPB) in FPGA #1 consists of Firewall and rate-limiting. Each security board has two gigabit port interface. Firewall module has two kinds of sub-module. Figure 2 depicts firewall sub modules.

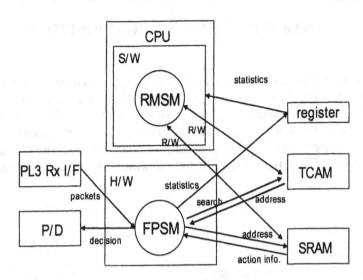

Figure 2 Design of firewall sub-modules

One is Filtering Process Sub-Module (FPSM) that is implemented on FPGA chip and the other is Rule Management Sub-Module (RMSM) that is software operating in embedded CPU.

2.1   Filtering Process Sub Module (FPSM)

FPSM makes decision whether the input packet should be permitted or dropped and is implemented using Verilog HDL. It uses one CYNSE 70256 TCAM for high speed rule searching and one SRAM to store action and statistic information. Each filtering rule match to action information in SRAM one to one. At first, FPSM receive input packets from PL3 Rx I/F and make key value for searching TCAM. Key value consists of Source IP, Destination IP, Source Port, Destination Port, Protocol, TCP Flags, ICMP header type, ICMP header code and so on. And FPSM get action information from SRAM using TCAM matching address founded by key value. Action information consist of 4 bits and are like following :

   bit 0 : if set '1' => permit
   bit 1 : if set '1' => block or drop
   bit 2 : if set '1' => Forensic port #0 gathering
   bit 3 : if set '1' => Forensic port #1 gathering

Both of bit 0 and bit 1 do not set at the same time but, others bits can be set concurrently. Statistic information on whether drop or permit are stored SRAM per filtering rules and those information are reported whenever user require.

Figure 3 depicts the processing of making decision whether the input packet should be permit or drop.

At first, if Key value of input packet does not matched to any rules in permission table, then the input packet is dropped. If matched to rule of permission, then it survey whether key value of input packet is matched to rules in blocking table again. If matched, the input packet is dropped but, if not matched, the packet is forwarded and copied.

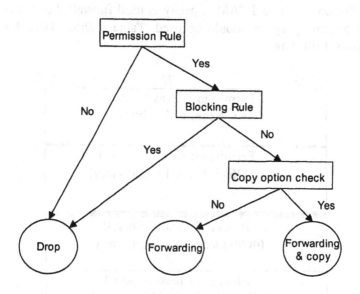

Figure 3: Processing of making decision

Permission Rule and blocking rule table are separated for effective filtering rule management. The reason why permission and blocking table are separated is not to make any conflicts between rules. For example, suppose that there are two kinds of rules like following and Rule 1 and Rule 2 applied at same table in order.

Rule 1 : Src IP (192.168.X.X) X means don't care
   : Dst IP (210.123.10.12)
   : Src Port (don't care)
   : Dst Port (80)
   : protocol (TCP)
<u>Action => Drop</u>
Rule 2 : Src IP (192.168.30.X) X means don't care
   : Dst IP (210.123.X.X)
   : Src Port (don't care)
   : Dst Port (80)
   : protocol (TCP)

<u>Action => Permit</u>

First match has priority in packet filtering matching. Accordingly, Packets which have source IP 192.168.30.X will be not permitted but blocked because the packet's key value matched to Rule 1. Manager can make rule properly that does not make conflict but, if there are thousands of rules, it's a heavy burden to manager.

TCAM capacity is 9Mbits (up to 128K entries in 72-bit configuration, up to 64k entries in 144-bit configuration) and is used for firewall and rate-limiting. So, only half of TCAM capacity is used firewall. For the filtering rule, 144-bit configuration should be used. Table 1 show TCAM address map for packet filtering.

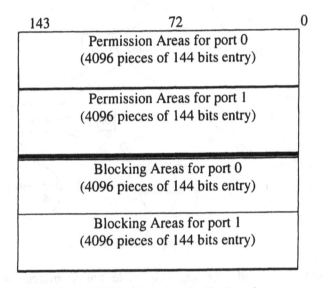

Table 1: TCAM address map for filtering rules.

2.2   Rule Management Sub Module (RMSM)

RMSM has the role of adding and deleting of filtering rules and has mirroring map of filtering tables in TCAM to manage filtering rules and also manage information of SRAM. Mirror map memory matched to TCAM address area is needed to manage filtering rules which are in hardware based TCAM because direct management of rules in hardware TCAM is restricted.

In case of adding new filtering rule, it should check whether the new rule is duplicated to already existing rule or not. If not, it finds empty entry area in TCAM mirror information in memory and add new rule to related location of TCAM and also add action information of new rule to related location of SRAM. When delete rule, it finds matched rule entry from TCAM mirroring information and delete entry in TCAM using index which gotten from mirroring information. Rule updating is similar to deleting. Rule management procedure is like following:

```
rule_management(){
if(add){
check whether already exists in mirror map;
find empty entry of mirror map;
add rule to TCAM using gotten index from mirror map;
add action info. to SRAM using gotten index from mirror map;
mirror map also added;
}
If(del){
 check whether deleting rule exists in mirror map;
 if not founded, error message and go to exit;
 delete the rule in TCAM using gotten index from mirror map;
 delete action info. in SRAM using gotten index from mirror map;
 delete the entry in mirror map;
}
}
```

Range matching and negation operation are also important in rule management because TCAM is basically exact matching device. In general, when manager make filtering rule, he may make port or IP range rules. Accordingly, one range rule should be divided to a large number of exact matching rules to support range matching. For example, port range from 1 to 3 can be transit to two rules that have port value binary "01" and binary "1x"(x means don't care bit) respectively. Separated permission and blocking tables are used for negation operation. For example, suppose that there is rule which drop packets except destination port 80 services. Then, the port 80 rule entry is added to permission table and the rule entry whose destination port field made by don't care is added blocking table.

3.   EXPERIMENTAL RESULTS

We have used IXIA Traffic Generator/Analyzer to generate and transmit packet to SGS. Security board of SGS has two gigabit interface fiber ports and two ports are connected to IXIA Traffic Generator. One port is used to receive packets from IXIA and the other port is used to send packets to IXIA again after processing. Even though network bandwidth is gigabit, the actual bandwidth depends on packet size. Table 2 shows actual bandwidth on each packet size. Two kinds of tests, for blocking and permission, have been done on three kinds of packet size. Filtering rules are also separated to 10, 100, and 1000 rules respectively.

Packet size	Actual bandwidth in Gigabit bandwidth environment
64 bytes	761 Mbps
256 bytes	927 Mbps
1500 bytes	986 Mbps

Table 2: Actual bandwidth on each packet size

At first, all blocking packets are generated and transmitted to SGS by IXIA. Table 3 shows that all packets are blocked regardless of the number of rules and packet size.

# of rules / packet size	10	100	1000
64 bytes	All blocked	All blocked	All blocked
256	All blocked	All blocked	All blocked
1500byte	All blocked	All blocked	All blocked

Table 3: Test results on blocking packets

Secondly, all accepting packets are generated and transmitted to SGS by IXIA. Table 4 shows that all packets are permitted regardless of the number of rules and packet size.

# of rules / packet size	10	100	1000
64 bytes	All permitted	All permitted	All permitted
256	All permitted	All permitted	All permitted
1500byte	All permitted	All permitted	All permitted

Table 4: Test results on permitting packets

Like test results, the number of rules has nothing to do with SGS system performance because Firewall is implemented in hardware. Actually, regardless of that the number of rules is 10 or 1000, TCAM rule searching is done from begin and end of TCAM address area.

4. CONCLUSION AND FUTURE WORK

In this paper, we have presented hardware based firewall for high performance network security. One of important requirements of security system is on high performance. Even though many security functions are supported, if not satisfied with network speed, those may not be used. We have developed security board which provides firewall function that support total 2 gigabit throughput (two gigabit ports).

Recently, most of firewall systems support not only static packet filtering but also dynamic packet filtering. Afterwards, we are going to add hardware based dynamic packet filtering.

References

[CZ95] Chapman, D. and Zwicky, E. "Internet Security Firewalls". O'Reilly, Sebastopol, Calf., 1995.

[Ken93] Kent, S. "Internet privacy enhanced mail". Commun. ACM 36, 8,(Aug. 1993),48-60

[Opp97] Rolf Oppliger. "Internet Security: Firewalls", Communication of the ACM, May,1997, Vol.40

[Wat02] "what to look for in next generation high-performance firewall appliances", www.watchguard.com, Nov. 2002.

[QVS01] Lili Qiu, George Varghese, Subhash Suri, "Fast firewall implementations for software-based and hardware-based routers", Proceedings of the 2001 ACM SIGMETRICS international conference on Measurement and modeling of computer systems, Volume 29 Issue 1

[SML04] Schuehler, D.V.; Moscola, J.; Lockwood, "Architecture for a hardware-based, TCP/IP content-processing system", IEEE , Volume: 24 , Issue: 1 , Jan.-Feb. 2004 ,Pages:62 - 69